Guitar for

Massimo Montarese

Beginners

D1379549

STERLING INNOVATION

An imprint of Sterling Publishing Co., Inc.

New York / London

www.sterlingpublishing.com

STERLING and the distinctive Sterling logo are registered trademarks of
Sterling Publishing Co., Inc.

New Chapter 1 art and Chapter 3 music and lyrics created by music typesetter
Robert L. Sherwin, The Farview Group, Inc. All other art is from the original Italian edition.
Photography by Michael Hnatov Photography with model Eric Hnatov

Translated from the Italian by Margaret Hatak
Guitar consultant and musical arrangements by Tamías ben-Magid

Library of Congress Cataloging-in-Publication Data
Montarese, Massimo.
  [Chitarra per tutti. English]
  Guitar for beginners / Massimo Montarese.
     p. cm.
  Originally published: Genoa : Artemisis Progetti Editoriali, 1996.
  Includes index.
  ISBN 1-4027-0945-5
  1. Guitar—Instruction and study. 2. Guitar—Methods—Self-instruction. I. Title.

MT588.M7913 2004
787.87'193--dc22

                                                                      2004019315

            2   4   6   8   10   9   7   5   3   1

Published by Sterling Publishing Co., Inc.
387 Park Avenue South, New York, NY 10016
Originally published in Italian under the title *La Chitarra per Tutti*
by Artemisia Progetti Editoriali in Genova, Italy
© by Nemo, via Dante, 2/96 16121 Genova
Translation and new material
© 2005 by Sterling Publishing Co., Inc.
Distributed in Canada by Sterling Publishing
c/o Canadian Manda Group, 165 Dufferin Street
Toronto, Ontario, Canada M6K 3H6
Distributed in the United Kingdom by GMC Distribution Services
Castle Place, 166 High Street, Lewes, East Sussex, England BN7 1XU
Distributed in Australia by Capricorn Link (Australia) Pty. Ltd.
P.O. Box 704, Windsor, NSW 2756, Australia

Sterling ISBN-13: 978-1-4027-5402-9
ISBN-10: 1-4027-5402-7

Contents

Introduction

When beginning to write a guide for students new to the guitar as well as for others who have been passionate about the instrument, I wanted to include not only the basics of music theory but a full explanation of the fundamental techniques for playing the guitar.

The guitar is firmly rooted in folk tradition, and written references to the guitar appeared as early as the 1300s. Music historians believe the instrument originated in Spain and was created by the people of Malaga. As the instrument evolved, its original four-course double strings were replaced by single strings, and in 1770 a sixth string was added. Unlike most other noble instruments, 20th century guitar maestros have been able to develop and codify their teachings with transcriptions from original texts. In the early 1800s, innovative composers and musicians, such as Fernando Sor (1778–1839) or Mauro Giulliani (1781–1829), helped make the guitar among the most esteemed instruments in the concert hall. Today we applaud the splendor of classical guitarist virtuosos like Andrés Segovia (1893–1987) as well as revolutionary electric guitar masters like Jimi Hendrix (1942–1970).

For everyone seriously interested in playing the instrument, classical guitar remains the reference point. However, other guitar-playing techniques and new repertoires continue to develop.

From African-American repertoires, traditional singer-songwriters, exasperated rock stars, and the archaic sounds of Celtic music that pass through the folk culture of Middle Earth, guitar canons and techniques found around the world have contributed much to our culture. This book organizes a series of exercises that can be simply executed by beginners. My goal is to invite readers to understand the principles that govern the instrument and to try these out through a series of exercises that eventually will make them feel at one with the guitar.

In the words of the celebrated jazz guitarist Fabio Mariani (b. 1962), "It is easy to learn the guitar the wrong way." It's important to carefully read all parts of this book and to practice the material daily. That's the best way to study guitar without wasting time. Finally, I hope that you'll soon understand more complex and evolved musical forms.

—Massimo Montarese

A Few Musical Notes

Before you begin to play, you'll need to understand basic music theory. Otherwise, you couldn't read the notes found on the musical staff. A few famous guitar players, like the late Django Reinhardt (1910–1953), did not read music, and many less accomplished musicians play by ear. To master the guitar, however, recognizing the complex structure of music will benefit your musicianship in both the short and long run.

If you're familiar with European solfège (Do–Re–Mi–Fa–Sol–La–Ti–Do) names of musical notes that Americans and Canadians usually call C–D–E–F–A–B–C, you'll be able to sing your way to more perfect notes as you pick out the tones on the guitar fingerboard. In the text of the first two chapters, the solfège notes appear in parentheses after the usual alphabetical designation for them. When presenting musical scales and other illustrations, we include solfège names next to the alphabetical ones when there's enough room.

Chapter 1
Music Theory Basics

How We Read & Write Music

For writing music, we use symbols for musical notes or tones on a grid that we call a *staff.* (The plural is *staffs* or *staves.)* The musical staff has five long horizontal lines with four spaces in between. It looks like this.

```
      5 ─────────────────────────────────────
lines 4 ─────────────────────────────────  4
      3 ─────────────────────────────────  3
      2 ─────────────────────────────────  2  spaces
      1 ─────────────────────────────────  1
```

Musical Staff

Symbols used for musical notes show us specific tones on the musical scale. In the musical staff below, we see notes sitting on the lines of the staff, and in the musical staff on page 8 (top), the notes sit in the spaces of the staff.

The name of each particular note is determined by a symbol called a *clef.* The clef appears at the beginning of each staff. The clef used for notating guitar music takes the name *treble clef* or *G clef.* Here's what the big "G" looks like:

You'll also recognize it on the staffs below. It defines the position (and pitch) of the note G (Sol) on the second line of the staff. This in turn establishes the position of the other notes, because they are relative to it.

Here are the notes on the *lines* of the musical staff in G clef, or the treble clef. They rise in position and tone from the lowest to the highest. It's easy to remember the letter names of the notes on these lines with the mnemonic **E**very **G**ood **B**oy **D**oes **F**ine.

Lines of the Musical Staff

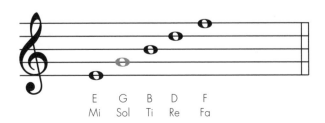

E   G   B   D   F
Mi   Sol Ti   Re   Fa

Here are the notes in the *spaces* of the musical staff in G clef. They rise in position and tone from the lowest to the highest. It's easy to remember the letter names of the notes in these spaces, because they spell **FACE**.

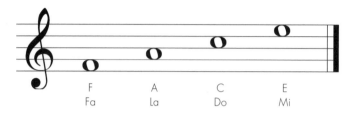

Spaces of the Musical Staff

Solfège   You may also be familiar with the European *solfège scale* that's often sung, Do–Re–Mi–Fa–Sol–La–Ti–Do. These are alternate names of musical notes we usually refer to by the letters C–D–E–F–G–A–B. The scale is the same. *Do* is *C,* followed by *Re* or *D,* and all other letters follow in progressively higher tones. It may help if you want to sing the scales to yourself to remember the tones. We've included the solfège scale in these early chapters in case you're more comfortable with it. We also refer to use of the solfège scale as *solmization,* exercises for the voice using syllables for tones on the musical scale.

From Low to High Notes

The notes on the lines and spaces of the musical staff create the gamut (range) of musical tones that rise from very *low* to very *high* according to *pitch.* On the guitar, the low strings refer to the *bass register,* and the high notes refer to the upper (in pitch) strings of the instrument.

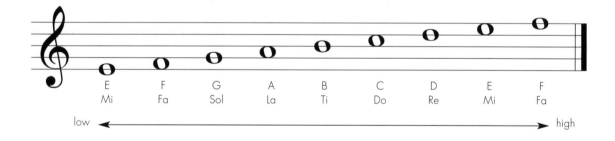

Notes on the Musical Staff

Notes on the musical staff can be on both lines and spaces. The notes rise from the lowest (beginning with the lowest line) to the highest pitch.

For notes pitched higher or lower than those on the musical staff, we add what are called *ledger lines* to help us visualize their appropriate positions and value, or pitch.

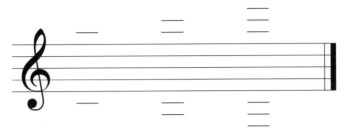

Adding Ledger Lines to the Musical Staff

The function of ledger lines is to extend the range of available tones. On the musical staff below, ledger lines extend the range of the C Major scale from one to two octaves. See how the musical notes can rise from the lower C (Do) to a C (Do) on the staff and finally, a high C (Do).

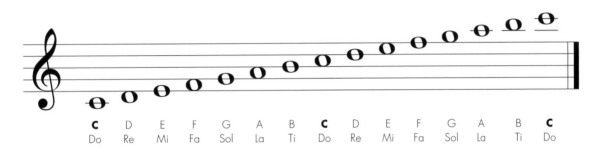

C	D	E	F	G	A	B	C	D	E	F	G	A	B	C
Do	Re	Mi	Fa	Sol	La	Ti	Do	Re	Mi	Fa	Sol	La	Ti	Do

Musical notes on ledger lines of the musical scale extend the musical scale two octaves.

If you know the how to sing the scale Do–Re–Me–Fa–Sol–La–Ti–Do, the European solfège system names of notes we call C–D–E–F–G–A–B–C, that will help you remember their rising tones or values.

Music Vocabulary

Pitch refers to the rate of vibration of a particular sound. Rapid vibrations create a high tone, and slow vibrations create a deep or low tone.

    Tone means a given fixed sound of a certain pitch. Tone also sometimes means the degree of distance, or the interval, between two sounds, such as that between a major and minor tone or a whole and semitone.

    The **clef** determines the name and pitch of the notes on the musical staff. We name the clef with a letter (C, F, or G). The clef, when prefixed to the musical staff, determines the pitch of the notes that follow. If the character is a G (Sol), we'd know that the music should be played in the G clef, with G (Sol) on the second to the bottom line of the staff.

Rhythmic Values, or the Beat

Rhythmic value, commonly called the *beat,* refers to the duration of musical tones within each bar (as distinct from their pitch values) and is indicated by the set of symbols we see below. They vary from the longest duration, a whole note, to the briefest, a sixty-fourth note.

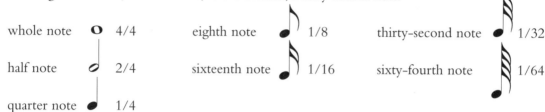

whole note   4/4   eighth note   1/8   thirty-second note   1/32

half note   2/4   sixteenth note   1/16   sixty-fourth note   1/64

quarter note   1/4

Rests

We also use symbols for the musical "silences," where we pause. These pauses are called *rests.* They can have the same duration as any of the beats above, so a rest may vary from a whole note to a sixty-fourth note in duration.

whole rest   4/4   eighth rest   1/8   thirty-second rest   1/32

half rest   2/4   sixteenth rest   1/16   sixty-fourth rest   1/64

quarter rest   1/4

We see both notes and rests juxtaposed below. The duration of a quarter note, for example, is the same as that for a quarter rest.

4/4   2/4   1/4   1/8   1/16   1/32   1/64

Clefs

Remember, the function of the *clef* is to indicate the available number of tones on the musical staff. Since it's impossible to express the totality of sounds within the range of one clef (that would require an inordinate number of ledger lines), different clefs are used to show the range of the voice or instrument being played. To play guitar, you need not learn the other clefs, but here are the others clefs you may look at for the sake of comparison. Guitar music is always in G clef, the treble clef.

Treble Clef, or G Clef

Bass Clef, or F Clef

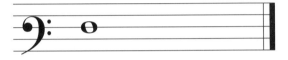

Baritone, or F Clef

C Clef, Soprano

C Clef, Mezzo Soprano

C Clef, Alto Clef

C Clef, Tenor Clef

The treble clef is used for the guitar, piano, violin, and many other instruments. Remember, guitar music will always appear in the treble clef.

The F clef, also known as the *bass clef,* is used both by opera or other bass singers, and more commonly, by pianists, for whom the clef indicates the piano left-hand portions of the score being played.

The F clef for the baritone has a different initial signature on the musical staff.

C Clef

For guitar, you won't need to know C clef. But this will help you understand how we write music. If you're interested in opera, this will be helpful. If not, just skip to page 12.

The *C clef, or alto clef,* is now used almost exclusively for the viola (also called the alto violin). It can also be found to some degree in the music of the English horn, trombone, and bassoon. It is pitched at *middle C,* that is, the C that divides the left hand from the right hand on the piano keyboard.

The C clef for the soprano, mezzo soprano, contralto (alto), and tenor can also be designated by the initial signatures of the musical staff.

Notice how the symbol for the C clef moves up or down the staff to indicate where the middle C (Do) appears. It's on the bottom line of the staff for soprano, the second from the bottom line for mezzo soprano, the third line for alto, and the fourth for tenor.

For operatic voices and musical instruments, a line may be added to the top or bottom of the musical staff to extend the range. If one is added to the top, one would be eliminated from the bottom and vice versa. The musical staff always shows only five lines.

Rhythm

Rhythm can be defined as a series of pulses expressed in regular time. These beats are indicated below on the musical staff. They are combined into *bars* or *measures* and graphically defined by vertical marks called *bar lines*. The numbers at the beginning of the staffs give us the number of beats per measure. Notice below that the first beat of every measure is stressed.

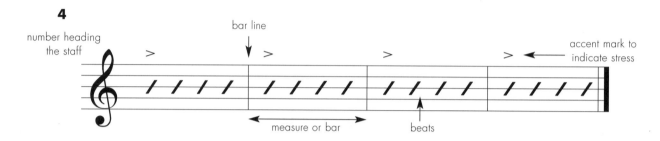

Each measure here has four beats; the first beat of each measure is stressed.

On a musical staff, a *bar* is the perpendicular line dividing one measure from another. Sometimes a measure is also called a bar, but this term strictly refers to the line itself.

The above example shows a series of four measures, each composed of four beats. Simpler configurations may have just two or three beats. Two-, three-, and four-beat measures are considered *simple rhythms*. Notice how the first beat of each measure in these examples is stressed.

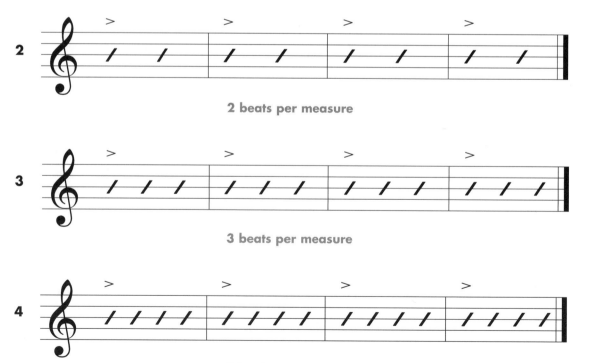

2 beats per measure

3 beats per measure

4 beats per measure

When we talk about 2/4, 3/4, or 4/4 rhythms, we mean measures that contain beats with the duration of quarter notes.

Other rhythms, such as 6/8, 9/8, and 12/8, shown below, we call *compound rhythms*. Here each quarter note has been divided into an eighth note, which determines how we count out the measure. Notice that there are six eighth notes in the first measure of *6/8 rhythm;* the same number appears in the second measure and so on. For *9/8 rhythm,* nine eighth notes are in each measure, and for *12/8 rhythm*, twelve eighth notes are in each measure.

Counting Out the Beat

Now let's apply what we've learned. Count the beats for each measure out loud and emphasize the first beat of each measure. Use your hand or foot to pound out the beat. Or clap your hands or say a syllable like "La" for each beat. A metronome will help you maintain a steady rhythm; just don't let the metronome become a crutch.

Try counting out loud and emphasizing the first beat of each measure of the *simple rhythms* 2/4 and 3/4.

For *compound rhythms*, we stress the first eighth note of each subdivision in each measure.

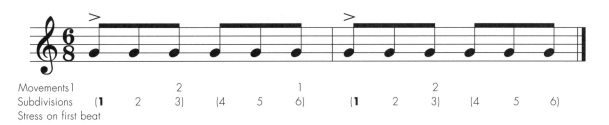

Notice the stress on the first eighth note of each measure and of each subdivision in 9/8 and 12/8 time.

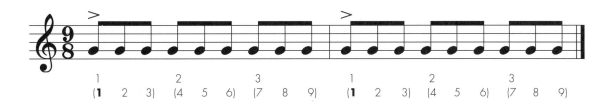

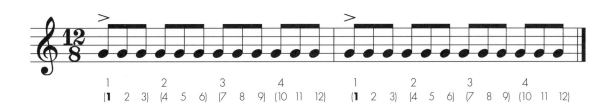

For *irregular* (i.e., composite) *rhythms,* like 5/4 and 7/8, we combine simple rhythms to create new ones. When counting them out, heed the additional stresses.

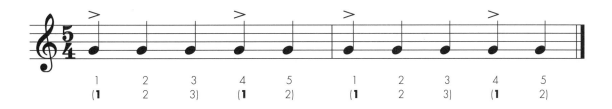

Remember that the fraction's top number (numerator) tells us the number of beats, and the bottom number (denominator) what the basic beat value is—i.e., quarter note, eighth note, or half note.

Common Time

Let's practice keeping a steady tempo, using the solfège scale and 4/4 time (common time). Say or sing each *solmization syllable* (Do, Re, or Mi, etc.) that appears under each note for the length the note (whole, half, or quarter) and the time signature (4/4) indicate.

The symbol 𝄴 may replace the fraction 4/4 to indicate *common time*.

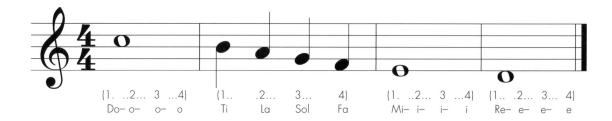

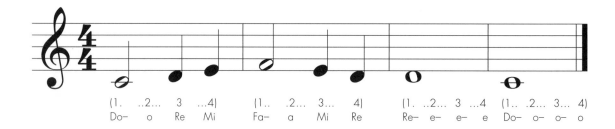

Flats, Sharps & Naturals

The smallest interval between two consecutive notes is a *semitone*. This corresponds to the distance between two successive frets on the guitar. When we want to heighten or lower these notes, we indicate that with a set of symbols, like the *sharp, flat, natural, double sharp,* or *double flat.* These symbols tell us that the natural notes have been altered in semitone (*half-step*) increments.

Modified Tones

♯   The **sharp sign** raises the note by a semitone.

♭   The **flat sign** lowers the note by a semitone.

♮   The **natural sign** restores an altered note to its natural state.

𝄪   The **double sharp** raises the note by a whole tone.

♭♭   The **double flat** lowers the note by a whole tone.

Tempo & Italian Music Vocabulary

Tempo, the Italian word for "time," usually means the speed of the music or of the rhythm—how quickly natural accents follow each other. Other Italian terms describe how fast or slow a piece of music should be played. From the slowest to the most rapid: *grave, largo, larghetto, adagio, lento, andante, andantino, moderato, allegretto, allegro, presto,* and *prestissimo.* Most of our language about music comes from Italian.

When grouped together just after the clef in a musical staff, these modified tones stand; that is, they become part of the key signature of the piece or song. When sharps, flats, or naturals appear individually, we call these notes *accidentals,* meant to be played only for the length of the measure. A natural sign cancels any previous alteration made within the measure.

Here are semitones found on the *chromatic scale.* The first staff shows notes in ascending order on the musical scale with associated sharps, and the second staff shows notes in descending order on the scale with associated flats.

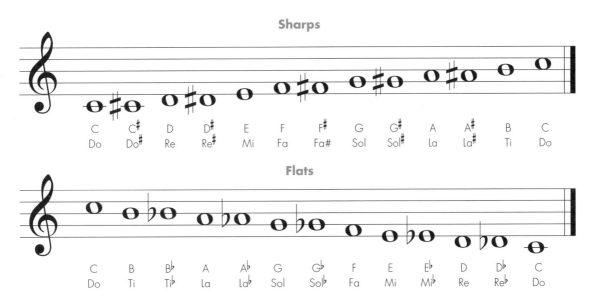

Notice how sharps are used going *up,* and flats appear going *down* the scale. Between the notes C (Do) and D (Re), you'll find the intermediate note C♯ (ascending) and D♭ (descending).

Thus, D♯ = E♭   (Re♯ = Mi♭)   F♯ = G♭   (Fa♯ = Sol♭)

        G♯ = A♭   (Sol♯ = La♭)   A♯ = B♭   (La♯ = Ti♭), etc.

Within the span of an *octave*—i.e., from the first C (Do) to the second C (Do)—there are twelve *half-steps* (or semitones) if we include all the accidentals. However, the intervals between E (Mi) and F (Fa), and between B (Ti) and C (Do), are by nature one semitone and do not, therefore, require additional sharps or flats.

Key Signature & Time Signature

Remember: The *key signature* heading the musical staff indicates the sharps and flats. The *time signature*, a fraction like 4/4, found at the head of a musical staff, may also appear where time changes within a musical composition. The time signature tells us how many beats per measure.

Musical Scale

The *musical scale* is a series of tones that begin with a fundamental note, or a *keynote* like C (Do), and ascend or descend until they complete an octave. Think of it as a ladder. The C scale corresponds to the model of the *diatonic major scale* with eight notes (degrees) and seven intervals in the order shown below.

C Scale (Key of C Major)

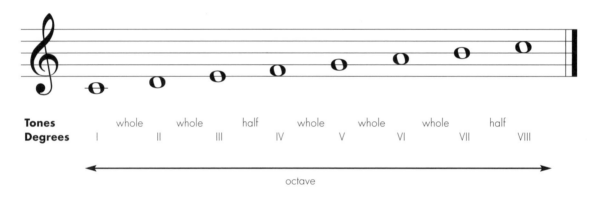

Whole tones and half-tones (semitones) found in an octave.

Each whole tone consists of two semitones. On the musical scale, you'll see the interval of a semitone (half-tone) between the third and fourth (III and IV) degrees as well as between the seventh and eighth (VII and VIII) degrees. Compare these intervals with those shown with sharps or flats.

The term *degree* refers to the step between two notes as well as to each line and space on the musical staff.

I. First degree tonic or fundamental
II. Second degree the supertonic
III. Third degree the mediant
IV. Fourth degree the subdominant

V. Fifth degree the dominant
VI. Sixth degree the submediant
VII. Seventh degree the subtonic or leading tone
VIII. Eighth degree the octave

Diatonic & Chromatic Scales

Remember, the **scale** is a succession or ladder of tones that may belong to any key. The two basic types are *diatonic* and *chromatic*. The **diatonic scale** may be major or minor; minor scales may in turn be natural, melodic, or harmonic. Major or minor (diatonic) scales alternate between whole and half-step tones (what we've called semitones). *Diatonic* means ascending or descending naturally through all *eight tones* of the octave of the major or minor scale. *Chromatic* means ascending or descending by semitones from a fundamental tone or tonic through its octave. The **chromatic scale** includes all the sharps and flats, or the half-tone (semitone) increments, making up a *twelve-tone scale*.

Intervals

The *interval* means the distance between two notes. Moving from notes C (Do) to F (Fa) brings us to a *fourth* interval (C-D-E-F or Do-Re-Mi-Fa). Intervals are defined not only numerically but qualitatively. We have five categories of intervals: *exact* (or *perfect*), *major, minor, diminished*, and *augmented*.

Perfect Intervals

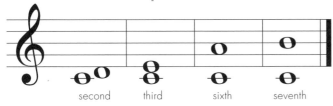

unison or prime   fourth   fifth   octave

Major Intervals

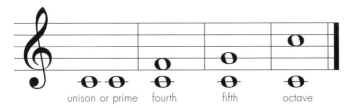

second   third   sixth   seventh

Minor Intervals

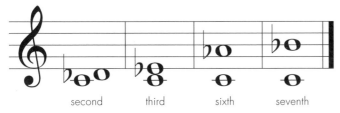

second   third   sixth   seventh

Diminished Intervals

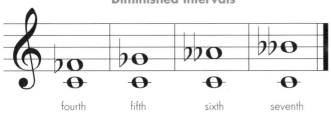

fourth   fifth   sixth   seventh

Augmented Intervals

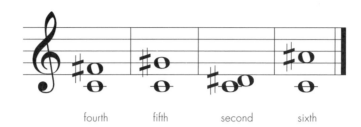

fourth   fifth   second   sixth

Let's look at the relationship between the kinds of intervals. In a major scale, beginning with the fundamental note (or tonic), there are four *major intervals,* C to D, C to E, C to A, C to B (Do to Re, Do to Mi, Do to La, Do to Ti), and three *perfect intervals,* C to F, C to G, C to C (Do to Fa, Do to Sol, Do to Do).

Minor intervals correspond to major intervals lowered by a semitone (half-step tone); *diminished intervals* are perfect intervals lowered by a half-tone; and minor intervals are lowered by the same degree. On the other hand, *augmented* major and perfect intervals *increase* by a semitone. These same intervals can exceed the octave range to make the ninth, tenth, eleventh, twelfth, and thirteenth.

Interval of the Ninth octave plus a major second.
That's C–D–E–F–G–A–B–C–D (Do–Re–Mi–Fa–Sol–La–Ti–Do–Re) or C to D of the succeeding octave.
Interval of the Tenth octave plus major third.
That's C–D–E–F–G–A–B–C–D–E (Do–Re–Mi–Fa–Sol–La–Ti–Do–Re–Mi) or C to E of the succeeding octave.
Interval of the Eleventh octave plus fourth.
That's C–D–E–F–G–A–B–C–D–E–F or C to F (Do–Re–Mi–Fa–Sol–La–Ti–Do–Re–Mi–Fa) C to F of the succeeding octave.
Interval of the Twelfth octave plus fifth.
That's C–D–E–F–G–A–B–C–D–E–F–G (Do–Re–Mi–Fa–Sol–La–Ti–Do–Re–Mi–Fa–Sol) or C to G of the succeeding octave.
Interval of the Thirteenth octave plus major sixth.
That's C–D–E–F–G–A–B–C–D–E–F–G–A (Do–Re–Mi–Fa–Sol–La–Ti–Do–Re–Mi–Fa–Sol–La) or C to A of the succeeding octave.

Inversions

We've considered the values of intervals in ascending order, where C to F (Do to Fa), for instance, in the ascent yields a fourth C–D–E–F (Do–Re–Mi–Fa). In descending from C to F (Do to Fa), however, we get a fifth C–B–A–G–F (Do–Ti–La–Sol–Fa). Continuing in descending order, here are the inversions.

Inversion of the *unison* note (or prime) corresponds to the *octave.*

Inversion of the *second* corresponds to the *seventh.*

Inversion of the *third* corresponds to the *sixth.*

Inversion of the *fourth* corresponds to the *fifth.*

Inversion of the *fifth* corresponds to the *fourth.*

Inversion of the *sixth* corresponds to the *third.*

Inversion of the *seventh* corresponds to the *second.*

Inversion of the *eighth* corresponds to the *first.*

Key Signatures—Tonality

We can use the C scale as the model of the *diatonic major scale.* Every diatonic major scale has the same relationsip of intervals. The interval between I and II degrees within an octave will always be a whole tone. Between II and III degrees is a whole tone, and between III and IV degrees is a half tone, etc.

The fundamental note or tonic of the scale is a sort of *center of sonic gravity.* Musicians call this a *tonality.* If the musical passage is in G major (Sol major), or the tonality of G major, we mean that the tones on the corresponding scale appear to have the fundamental note G (Sol) as their center. The tones also respect the scale's structure of intervals (seen on page 18).

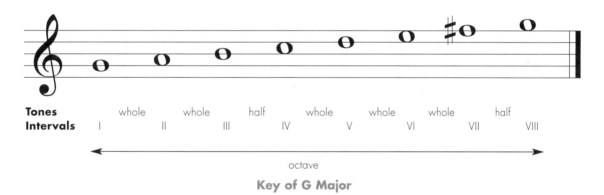

| **Tones** | whole | whole | half | whole | whole | whole | half |
| **Intervals** | I | II | III | IV | V | VI | VII | VIII |

octave

Key of G Major

To indicate the *key signatures* on the staff, we write the appropriate number of sharps and flats after the clef (see page 23). This alerts us to the notes on the scale we must make sharp or flat as well as those we sound unaltered. The staff above tells us that all F's (Fa's) will be sharp. Whether or not they have sharps or flats, all major scales are constructed on the same principle.

Remember that *accidentals*—other sharps, flats, and naturals—may later be introduced apart from the signature. But here we're concerned with the key signature.

Keynote

The **keynote** is the first note of a musical scale. It also means the harmonically fundamental tone of a scale. We build chords on the fundamental note. We can also call this note the chief or ground note, or the tonic.

Scales with Sharps

Here are the scales for six key signatures that may be positioned after the G clef. Notice the *sharps* we would find in various keys. Find Key of C# on page 25.

Here's how we express the sharps as part of the *key signature*, just after the symbol for G clef. Notice that with each measure below we've added a new sharp. The key signatures correspond to each of the scales found on page 22.

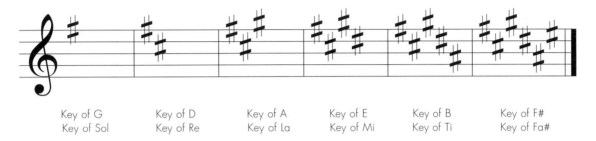

Key of G   Key of D   Key of A   Key of E   Key of B   Key of F#
Key of Sol   Key of Re   Key of La   Key of Mi   Key of Ti   Key of Fa#

Let's compare the scale of C (Do) major (**Do**-Re-Mi-Fa-Sol-La-Ti-Do) to the first altered scale, i.e., the scale of G (Sol) (**Sol**-La-Ti-Do-Re-Mi-Fa-Sol). We observe that, starting from the *dominant of C* (Do), which is G (Sol), we obtain a new scale with modifications that give it a particular character. The scales on page 22 appear to follow this rule: From the fifth degree (V) of each diatonic major scale, we can construct a new one that will contain one newly altered note as well as those preceding. This *last* will always be the *leading tone of the new scale.*

We've seen the tonalities generated through *sharps.* Now let's look at those derived from *flats.*

Scales with Flats

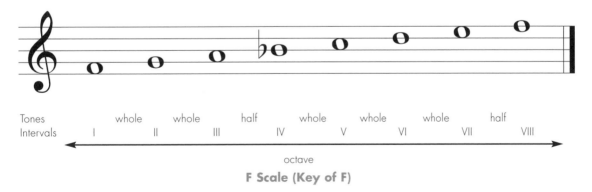

Tones		whole	whole	half	whole	whole	whole	half
Intervals	I	II	III	IV	V	VI	VII	VIII

octave

F Scale (Key of F)

If we study the F (Fa) scale above and keep in mind how it is related to the scale of C (Do) major, we'll see how to find this F scale. We begin with the *subdominant of C* (Do), which is F (Fa), the IV degree, and make it flat through the leading tone, B (Ti).

Here's the rule: From every subdominant of a scale that is IV above or V below, if we make a half-tone (or semitone) flat we'll create the leading tone of the scale that comes before.

On page 24 are the flats we would find in six keys. For Key of C♭ see page 25.

Scales with Flats

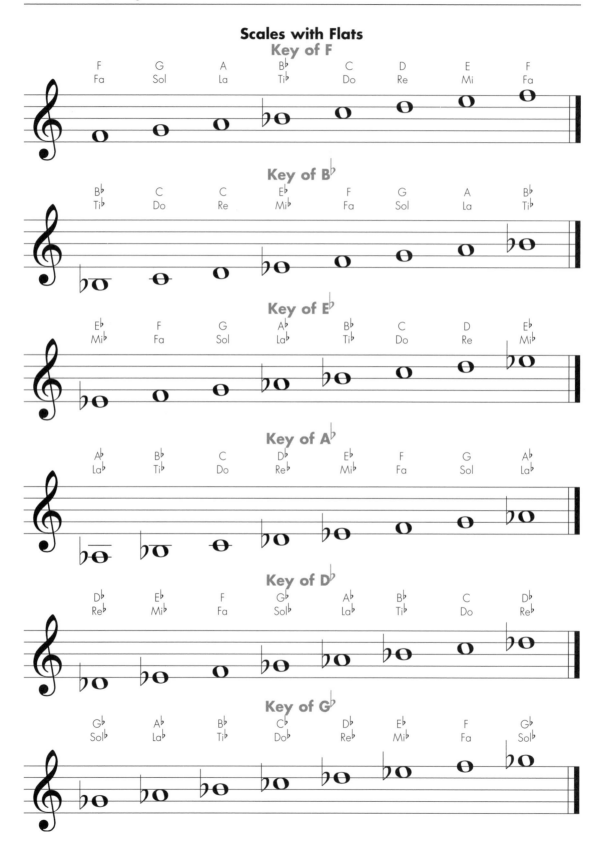

For the scales with flats on page 24, here are the *key signatures* that follow the symbol for G clef.

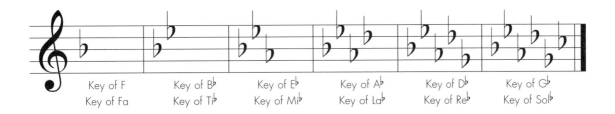

Key of F   Key of B♭   Key of E♭   Key of A♭   Key of D♭   Key of G♭
Key of Fa   Key of Ti♭   Key of Mi♭   Key of La♭   Key of Re♭   Key of Sol♭

In the scale of C♯ (Do♯) and C♭ (Do♭) we have all of the altered notes.

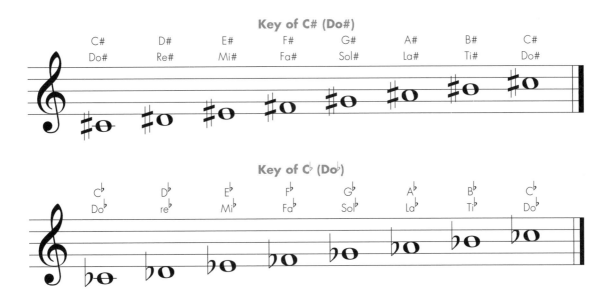

Major and Minor Modes

In the *major mode,* the third degree from the keynote forms a *major interval*. In the *minor mode,* the third degree from the keynote forms a *minor interval*.

Remember how the diatonic major scale (see page 18) is constructed. In that scale an interval of two whole tones between the tonic and the mediant (defined as a major third) give the scale its peculiar character. Beginning at the sixth (VI) degree of the major scale, we obtain a new one with a different order of intervals. The interval between tonic and mediant (a minor third) will be a tone and a half, which defines the new scale as a *natural minor*.

The *mediant* is the third note of the scale; it's the middle note between the tonic and the dominant.

A Natural Minor Scale

Tones		whole		half		whole		whole		half		whole		whole	
Intervals	I		II		III		IV		V		VI		VII		VIII

octave

A Minor Harmonic Scale

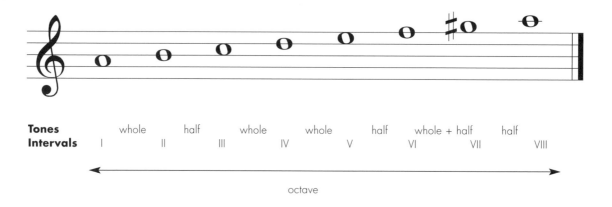

Tones		whole		half		whole		whole		half		whole + half		half	
Intervals	I		II		III		IV		V		VI		VII		VIII

octave

To match the interval between the seventh (VII) and eighth (VIII) degrees with the corresponding interval in the major mode (one semitone), the note G (Sol) becomes sharp, thereby attaining what we call the *harmonic minor scale*.

A Minor Melodic Scale, Ascending

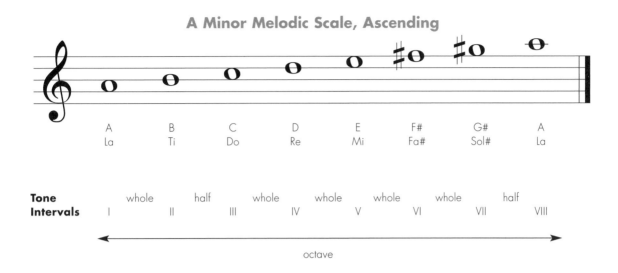

	A	B	C	D	E	F#	G#	A
	La	Ti	Do	Re	Mi	Fa#	Sol#	La

Tone Intervals		whole	half	whole	whole	whole	whole	half	
	I		II		III		IV		V		VI		VII		VIII

octave

Because we desire a more uniform sound, we insert a one-and-a-half-tone interval between the sixth (VI) and seventh (VII) degrees, thereby introducing the *ascending melodic minor scale.* For this scale, we alter notes *only* as we go up the scale and return to the relative minor notes as we go down the scale.

A Minor Melodic Scale, Descending

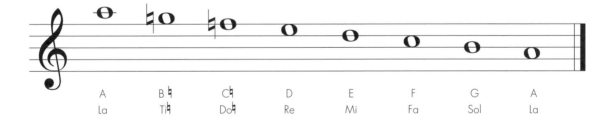

	A	B♮	C♮	D	E	F	G	A
	La	Ti♮	Do♮	Re	Mi	Fa	Sol	La

Notice how the sharps become *naturals* when descending the scale.

Triads

Until now, we have been dealing with the melodic aspect of music, sounds that are conceived as single notes on a scale. However, on the guitar (just as on the piano, another instrument capable of producing harmonies), we can play several notes simultaneously following a given tempo. Therefore, we need to know the rules that govern relationships between tones to be able to understand, even in a simple way, how to form chords. The term *triad* means a blending of three musical pitches in intervals of thirds set one atop the other. Beginning with the fundamental tone of the C Major (Do Major) scale, we obtain the triadic structure (I) of C-E-G (Do-Mi-Sol).

Using this model, let's continue to construct a triad upon each note of the major scale.

D-F-A	**E**-G-B	**F**-A-C	**G**-B-D	**A**-C-E	**B**-D-F
Re-Fa-La	**Mi**-Sol-Ti	**Fa**-La-Do	**Sol**-Ti-Re	**La**-Do-Mi	**Ti**-Re-Fa
II	III	IV	V	VI	VII

We can place these triads on the staff.

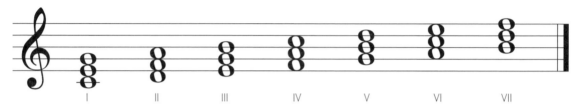

Triads of the Harmonic Minor Scale

On the same general principle, let's construct the triads of the *harmonic minor scale.*

A-C-E	**B**-D-F	**C**-E-G#	**D**-F-A	**E**-G#-B	**F**-A-C	**G#**-B-D
La-Do-Mi	**Ti**-Re-Fa	**Do**-Mi-Sol#	**Re**-Fa-La	**Mi**-Sol#-Ti	**Fa**-La-Do	**Sol#**-Ti-Re

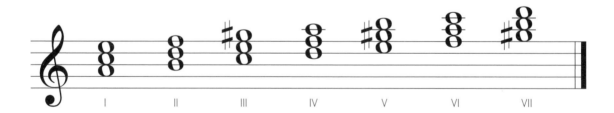

Triads: Major, Minor, Augmented & Diminished

Although derived from the same scale, notice how different these triads are from those preceding, especially in their harmonization. It is important to study the theory supporting the examples of triads shown on page 29, the significance of the intervals that compose them, and the scale relationships from which they derive. Notice, if you will, the four kinds of triads: major, minor, augmented, and diminished.

Major Triads	I	2 tones (or steps)	III	1½ steps	V
Minor Triads	I	1½ steps	III	2 steps	V
Augmented Triads	I	2 steps	III	2 steps	V
Diminished Triads	I	1½ steps	III	1½ steps	V

We build individual triads, like those on page 28, on the major and minor scales. If we observe the Major Scale and the Harmonic Minor Scale models below, with their sequence of steps or tones, we can better understand how triads are created.

Major Scale

Degree	Model with steps or tones						Triad
I	C (Do)	2 steps (tones)	E (Mi)	1½ steps	G (Sol)		Major
II	D (Re)	1½ steps	F (Fa)	2 steps	A (La)		Minor
III	E (Mi)	1½ steps	G (Sol)	2 steps	B (Ti)		Minor
IV	F (Fa)	2 steps	A (La)	1½ steps	C (Do)		Major
V	G (Sol)	2 steps	B (Ti)	1½ steps	D (Re)		Major
VI	A (La)	1½ steps	C (Do)	2 steps	E (Mi)		Minor
VII	B (Ti)	1½ steps	D (Re)	1½ steps	F (Fa)		Diminished

Harmonic Minor Scale

Degree	Model with steps or tones						Triad
I	A (La)	1½ steps (tones)	C (Do)	2 steps	E (Mi)		Minor
II	B (Ti)	1½ steps	D (Re)	1½ steps	F (Fa)		Diminished
III	C (Do)	2 steps	E (Mi)	2 steps	G$^\sharp$ (Sol$^\sharp$)		Augmented
IV	D (Re)	1½ steps	F (Fa)	2 steps	A (La)		Minor
V	E (Mi)	2 steps	G$^\sharp$ (Sol$^\sharp$)	1½ steps	B (Ti)		Major
VI	F (Fa)	2 steps	A (La)	1½ steps	C (Do)		Major
VII	G$^\sharp$ (Sol$^\sharp$)	1½ steps	B (Ti)	1½ steps	D (Re)		Diminished

Chords derive from triads. We'll discuss more complicated chords in a later chapter.

Within each major scale (see page 29), we expect to find this succession of chords.

I	major chord
II	minor chord
III	minor chord
IV	major chord
V	major chord
VI	minor chord
VII	diminished chord

Within each harmonic minor scale, we will find this succession of chords.

I	minor chord
II	diminished chord
III	augmented chord
IV	minor chord
V	major chord
VI	major chord
VII	diminished chord

Now that we've talked about music theory and have a basic understanding of scales and primary chord structures, let's consider the very practical matter of how to tune and handle the guitar.

Chapter 2

Tuning & Playing the Guitar

Guitars have evolved over the centuries, and new variations and hybrids always seem to be popping up. But all are derived from three basic types: (1) the classic guitar, (2) the solid- or hollow-bodied electric guitar, and (3) the standard 6- or 12-string folk guitar. Take a minute to get acquainted with your own guitar's structure by looking carefully at the diagrams on page 32 (classic) or page 33 (electric). This book focuses on the six-string guitar.

The classical guitar is the oldest, and it offers the greatest repertoire and formalized playing techniques. Many popular musicians have begun their careers by mastering at least some of them. It's not nearly as difficult as some imagine to transfer these standard techniques from one instrument to another; there's actually a good deal of overlap, as recorded music attests. The chief difference between the classical guitar and the others is that the former is always played seated and never with any kind of plectrum. Also, strings made for each type of guitar are *not* interchangeable—these peculiarities must be respected. It may please you to learn, though, that however different the particulars of their construction, all guitars are tuned in exactly the same way. This is the first thing we need to learn.

Tuning the Guitar

To properly tune the guitar, we need either another musical instrument or an external device that emits the note A (La) at 440 Hz. (The abbreviation *Hz* stands for "hertz," a term in physics indicating a unit of frequency equal to one cycle per second.) This is often called *concert A*. Therefore, we can use a piano (assuming it is in tune) or keyboard synthesizer, a tuning fork, a pitch pipe, or an *electronic tuner*. Any of these will supply us with the correct pitch (or digital readout if you're using an electronic tuner) for tuning the open A string (the fifth string), with which we always begin. Adjust the tuning peg on this string and pluck it until the two tones correspond in pitch. After that's done, you'll tune the remaining strings from the guitar itself. Press the now-tuned A string firmly just behind the fifth fret and pluck it so that you hear the tone you need to tune the next string (the 4th), which is the open D (Re) string. Then repeat this last operation, again on the fifth fret, with this string, in order to hear the note G (Sol).

Classical Guitar

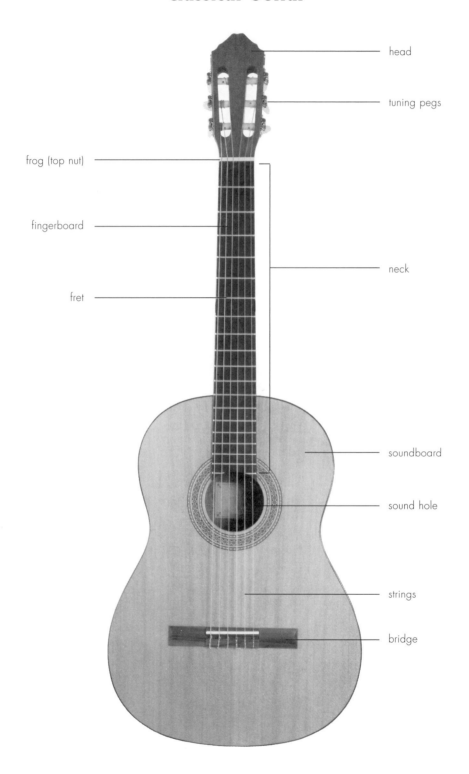

head

tuning pegs

frog (top nut)

fingerboard

fret

neck

soundboard

sound hole

strings

bridge

Electric Guitar

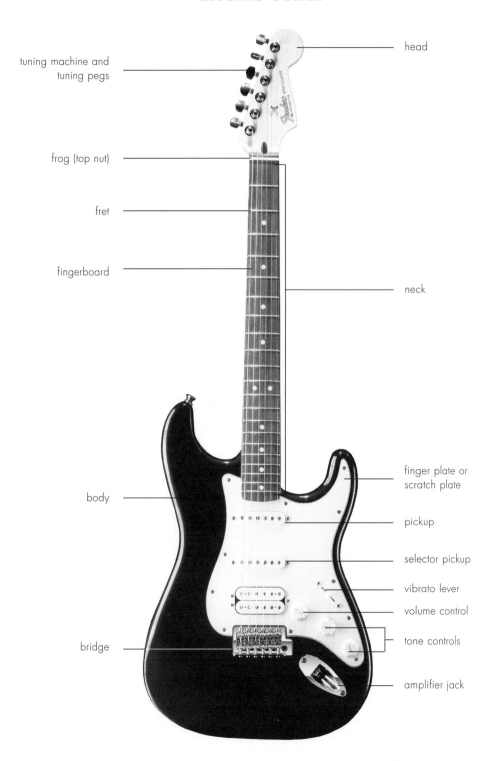

tuning machine and
tuning pegs

head

frog (top nut)

fret

fingerboard

neck

finger plate or
scratch plate

body

pickup

selector pickup

vibrato lever

volume control

tone controls

bridge

amplifier jack

When you tune the second string, B (Ti), you must press down behind the *fourth* fret on the third string, G (Sol), because the distance between the G and B strings is a major third, not a fourth as between the other strings. With the B string now in tune, once again press down on it behind the fifth fret in order to hear the upper E (Mi). Be careful tuning the last two high strings. You need to do it slowly and gradually because they are thinner than the other strings and have a tendency to break more easily. It might take a few tries to get the proper knack. Don't worry if you snap a few strings at first; it happens to everyone.

After the high E is tuned, use the latter to adjust the E string in the bass register, which is two octaves lower. This way of tuning the sixth string is helpful in developing your pitch sense. While using an electronic tuner to pitch all the strings is convenient, the old tried-and-true method is more beneficial. Tuning a guitar may seem simple, but it takes constant practice to develop the musical sensitivity necessary to hear the subtle differences between the various strings. However, doing so allows you to tune accurately.

To see how the notes of the tuned guitar look on the staff—going from low E (Mi) to high E (Mi) on the open strings, see page 42. The high E of the guitar is sometimes referred to as the *chanterelle.*

Playing Positions

Both folk and electric guitars can be fitted with shoulder straps, so that you can play standing up. The classical guitarists play in a seated position, resting the guitar on the left thigh and cradling it, as it were, between the legs (see photo right). Lift the left heel a bit, resting the foot on the ball, so that the left leg is slightly higher than the right. You want the tuning head to be at the same level or slightly lower than your left shoulder; try both positions to find out which is more comfortable for you. When playing in a standing position, make sure to adjust the shoulder strap correctly, giving you the same guitar position you'd have if seated.

Hand positions must be relaxed and neither too firm nor too loose, but so that you can move them properly and execute the music. For the left hand, imagine that the neck of the guitar has a line that runs at midpoint down its length. That's where the thumb should remain; try not to let it slip over the top edge. The playing fingers hang perpendicularly over the strings in conjunction with the frets and fingerboard. To avoid the buildup of tension in execution, other parts of the hand should not come into contact with the neck; such shortcuts will impede progress in study.

The *right hand*, whether picking out notes or plucking arpeggiated chords, should hover over the strings in readiness without additional support from the body of the guitar. This position can be maintained only when the right forearm is supported on the rounded upper portion of the instrument (as in the classical stance). When using a plectrum, keep the forearm parallel to the soundboard, moving the pick up and down on the strings while grasping it firmly between index finger and thumb.

Note: In the classical style, we simply alternate the fingers. In other words, the same string is never played twice with the same finger. (Also see Chapter 6, "Using the Right Hand.")

Classical position.

Placement of fingers on fingerboard.

Left-hand position on the neck.

T   thumb
I   index finger
M   middle finger
R   ring finger

Fingers of the Right Hand   We use the initials T, I, M, and R to denote the fingers of the right hand. We don't include the little finger.

Picking   We'll borrow symbols from violinists that indicate how to move the pick on the strings.

П   downward motion of the pick   **V**   upward motion of the pick

Guitar Fingering Exercises

Warm-Up Right-Hand Exercises

This initial exercise, though simple, will familiarize you with the open strings. (By *open strings,* we mean no frets are used to hold down any strings.) Refer to photos in this chapter before you begin. Alternate the index and middle fingers or use the up-and-down motion of a pick for this warm-up exercise.

* Play each open string, going from high to low, four times. Repeat.
* Play each open string two times, this time going from low to high. Repeat.
* Going from high to low, play each open string one time. Repeat.
* Going from low to high, play each open string one time. Repeat.

Left-Hand Exercises for Fretted Tones

Now let's create our first fretted tones, keeping in mind that for the left hand, we use the appropriate fingers for each fret.

* The first, or index, finger presses down the strings on the **first fret.**
* The second, or middle, finger presses down the strings on the **second fret.**
* The third, or ring, finger presses down the strings on the **third fret.**
* The fourth, or pinky or little, finger presses down the strings on the **fourth fret.**

Basic Exercise

Begin with this basic exercise.

* Sound an open string. Then press down the same string behind the **first fret.**
* Sound another open string. Then press down the same string behind the **second fret.**
* Sound another open string. Then press down the same string behind the **third fret.**
* Sound any other open string. Then press down the same string behind the **fourth fret.**

Now play all four tones for each string **in sequence,** going up and down the frets one semitone at a time. *Remember to change fingers in respect to the frets as you do so!* Repeat this exercise until it's fluid.

Right hand with pick.

Position of electric guitar when fitted with shoulder strap. You can also stand.

Right hand holding a pick. Picks are also called flatpicks, plectrums, or plectra.

Arpeggios

Arpeggios are simply chords whose individual notes are sounded out in quick succession, starting with the low notes and going up to higher notes, or going down the scale from high to lower notes. With the left hand holding down a chord on the fingerboard, the pick or thumb strokes the notes of the bass strings (the sixth, the fifth, and the fourth) while the index finger plucks any notes on the third string, the middle finger the second, and the ring finger the first.

Any chord can be played as an arpeggio, but first you'll need to learn how to read chord diagrams. (See Chapter 6 for more details.)

Reading Chord Diagrams

C Major Chord

Chord diagrams represent the top nut (or frog), frets, and strings on the guitar. The thick black vertical line on the far left indicates the *top nut* and the thin vertical lines the *frets*, raised metal strips placed at intervals along the fingerboard of the neck of the guitar. The horizontal lines that vary in thickness represent the *strings* and show their position on the guitar. Each string sounds a different note or tone. From the thinnest to the thickest string are E–B–G–D–A–E (Mi–Ti–Sol–Re–La–Mi); we've numbered them 1 to 6 (see page 39).

The Six Strings of the Guitar

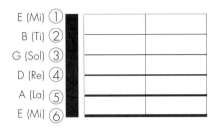

Top Nut The top nut is the thick black line at the left of the top diagram on page 38 and on the above diagram on this page. It appears before the first fret on the neck of the guitar.

Frets These are shown as thin vertical lines, and fret positions are marked by roman numerals (below the strings just before the fret itself).

Strings These horizontal lines vary in thickness from the thickest at the bottom to the thinnest at the top and represent how the strings are arranged on the neck of a guitar. The strings are also called the E (Mi) or first string (the thinnest string at the top of our diagram), B (second string), G (Sol) or third string, D (Re) or fourth string, A (La) or fifth string, and E (Mi) or sixth string (the thickest string at the bottom of our diagram).

Open Strings Sounding Notes When the string is *open,* that is, when it is sounded without being fretted, we indicate this with a "O" beside the string on the chord diagram.

Strings Not Played If the string does not have to be played, we indicate this with an "X" beside the string on the chord diagram. See the top chord diagram on page 38 for both the open strings "O" and strings not played "X."

1 index finger
2 middle finger
3 ring finger
4 little finger or pinky

Fingers Left-hand fingerings, used to hold down the frets, are indicated by the black numbered circles shown left, which are positioned on their respective strings on the chord diagram.

Barré The barré is a thin line that spans the width of the fingerboard and is attached to two numbered circles that show the finger used to achieve it. (See VIII fret in the second chord diagram on page 38.) Press down firmly just behind the fret in order to avoid losing any of the notes making up the chord. This takes practice, but it's important to master this technique.

Notes on the Guitar's Fingerboard

Becoming familiar with all the notes on the guitar fingerboard will speed your progress as a student of guitar. One way to do this is by playing scales in all keys along its entire length. You'll find the musical scales in the next chapters, but first carefully study the detailed chart of the fingerboard on this page. We show the full range of the fingerboard with the musical notes for given strings for the twelve frets on the neck of the guitar. (Frets thirteen (XIII) to twenty-four (XXIV) repeat the notes in the higher ranges.) In your study, you'll want to return to this diagram again and again. Your actual finger positions, as you see, will be between the frets, the raised metal strips placed at intervals along the fingerboard. These metal strips are represented below as thin vertical lines.

Roman numerals indicate the twelve frets. Remember that you play these notes just above the numbered fret. (Or rather where you'd sound the notes on the strings just above the numbered frets.)

We've indicated the six strings of the guitar, the E, B, G, D, A, and E strings (shown horizontally) beside the thick bold vertical line that's the frog (top nut) just before the guitar's fingerboard. From the thinnest E string, to the second thinnest (B string), third string (G string), fourth string (D string), the fifth string (A string), to the sixth and thickest (another E string). When we talk about an open A string, for instance, we're talking about the fifth string. Don't confuse an A note with an A string.

For example, for fret I (found below the frog or top nut and above fret I), you'd be able to play F on the thickest and thinnest strings as shown, while you'd find A# and B♭ on the second thickest string (with A# above B♭), D# just above E on the third thickest string, G# just above A♭ on the fourth thickest string, and C in the middle of the fifth thickest string.

When presenting the musical scales, such as C Major, we also show those portions of the fingerboard needed for playing selected scales. What we show begins with the first fret (I), then the second (II), and so on, unless otherwise indicated with the appropriate roman numeral. Chord diagrams on the fingerboard are also set up this way.

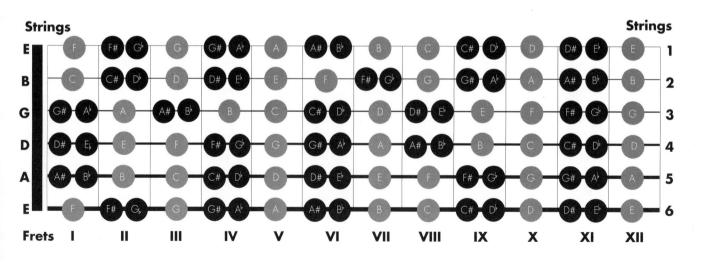

CHAPTER 3
Scales, Chords & Song Selections

In this chapter we present the major and minor musical scales along with their fingering positions on the guitar fingerboard. We begin with the Key of C Major and end with the Key of G♭ (or F♯ Major). For each key, we've introduced a traditional popular song preceded by chord diagrams and rhythm charts to help you learn to play each song. We've also included the lyrics, though perhaps not the ones you're most familiar with since traditional songs have many versions and variations. You'll find twelve songs: "All Through the Night," "Amazing Grace," "The Ash Grove," "Drink to Me Only with Thine Eyes," "Greensleeves," "Hark! The Herald Angels Sing," "House of the Rising Sun," "Oh, Mary, Don't You Weep," "My Country, 'Tis of Thee" ("God Save the Queen"), "Scarborough Fair," "Spanish Is a Loving Tongue," and "The Water Is Wide."

Musical Scales   The musical scales show the tones (C–D–E–F–G–A–B–C) found within an octave on the staff. When space permits, we also give the solfège for the same tones (Do–Re–Mi–Fa–Sol–La–Ti–Do). Sharps and flats appear where necessary. Fingering positions on the guitar fingerboard are given for two-octave scales. Guitar students should memorize all the scales.

Fingerboard   We show you how to find your finger positions on the guitar's fingerboard to play the tones (sound the notes) of the particular musical scale. Begin with the lowest tone and lowest string in the appropriate fret as indicated. Also review the fuller fingerboard chart on page 40.

For example, to play the tone or note C in the Scale of C Major (page 44), you'd play the thickest (lowest or E string) on the eighth fret of the fingerboard. The dark circle "4" reminds you to play this note with your little finger. Next you'll find the D on the A string (next thickest string) in the fifth fret, and the dark circle "1" suggests that you play this with your index finger. On the same (A) string, you'd then find the E at the seventh fret and the F at the eighth fret. You'll find the G on the D string (third thickest string) at the fifth fret, the A on the same string at the seventh fret, and so on. Just a helpful hint: Remember, the thinner the string, the higher the note, and the shorter the string (the closer you are to the guitar's soundboard hole), the higher the tone or note.

Chord Diagrams   We supply chord diagrams to help you learn the popular songs we've chosen here. For instance, on page 45 you'll see chord diagrams for the song "Oh, Mary, Don't You Weep." You'll find the chord for G with three open strings (marked on the far left of the diagram beside the thick bold line with an "O" beside each open string), and the finger positions (2 for the middle finger, 3 for the ring finger, 4 for the little finger or pinky) used to play the notes making up the chord on the appropriate strings within the appropriate frets. For the G chord, you'd play the A string (fifth string or second thickest), which is open because it's marked with an "O," within the second fret. You'd also play the E string (sixth string or thickest string) with finger 3 (ring finger) and the other E string (first string or thinnest string) with finger 4 (little finger). We know that the strings for the two E strings are not "open" because no "O" appears beside the thick far left line on the chord diagram.

Don't forget that you'll be playing all three notes at the same time to produce the chord. To figure out the specific notes played within a given chord, again refer to the fingerboard chart on page 40 at the end of Chapter 2. For the G chord, for instance, finger 2 (middle finger) plays note B (fifth or A string within the second fret), finger 3 (ring finger) plays note G (sixth or E string within the third fret), and finger 4 (little finger) plays the higher note G (first or E string within the third fret).

Rhythm Charts   Each song is preceded by a rhythm chart to show the beats or how you'd strum or pluck the guitar strings with your right hand while playing each chord with your left hand. Rhythm charts are also helpful for learning the harmonic progression for singing that song. You could also use a metronome, if you wish. The appropriate chords for the song appear above the musical staff of the rhythm chart. For the song "Oh, Mary, Don't You Weep" (rhythm chart on page 45), you'd begin in the first staff, first bar with a G chord for four beats. In the second bar, you'd change to a D chord for four beats, and in the third bar you'd play a D7 chord for four beats, etc. In the second staff, (first bar) you'd play a C chord for four beats; (second bar) a G chord for four beats; (third bar) a G chord for two beats and a D chord for two beats; and finally (fourth bar) a G chord for four beats. To find the appropriate fingering for the chords on the fingerboard, consult the chord diagrams also on page 45 for the song "Oh, Mary, Don't You Weep." The chords shown are for G, D, D7, and C.

Song Selections   Music and lyrics follow the chord diagrams and rhythm charts for selected songs drawn from English, Welsh, and American folk traditions. The melodies appear in standard music notation with chords named above the staffs. Tamías ben-Magid has slightly revised traditional arrangements for guitar.

Guitar Strings   Here's how the notes on the tuned guitar would appear on the musical staff, going from low E (Mi) to high E (Mi) on the open strings. The high E on the guitar is sometimes referred to as the *chanterelle*.

Strings	E	A	D	G	B	E
	Mi	La	R	So	Ti	Mi
Strings	6	5	4	3	2	1

Scale of C Major

Scale of C Major

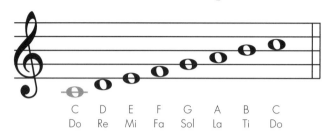

Fingerboard

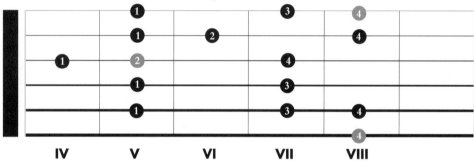

Fingering positions for scale extended over two octaves, shown on the fingerboard, beginning on the fourth fret.

Scale of A Harmonic Minor

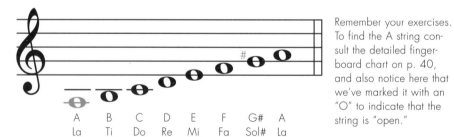

Remember your exercises. To find the A string consult the detailed fingerboard chart on p. 40, and also notice here that we've marked it with an "O" to indicate that the string is "open."

Fingerboard

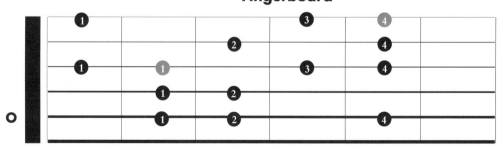

Begin on the (open) A string.

Chord Diagrams for "Oh, Mary, Don't You Weep"

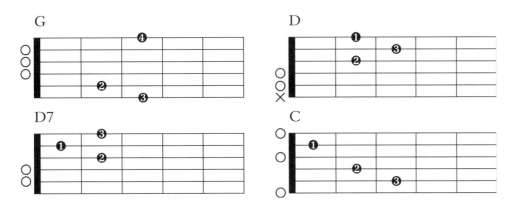

Using these chord diagrams, learn the appropriate chords in sequence. First apply the fingerings. When you're able to move easily from one chord to another, use a simple strumming pattern to get the "feel" of the accompaniment. Then, whether or not you know the song's melody, work it out first on the guitar's fingerboard (see page 40), learning the lyrics as you go along. The process will become easy and natural with practice, although it would be best to have an experienced guitarist guide you.

Rhythm Chart for "Oh, Mary, Don't You Weep"

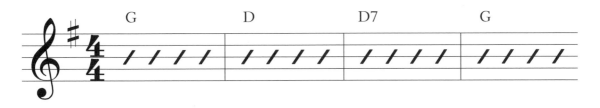

Oh, Mary, Don't You Weep

American spiritual

Oh, Ma – ry, don't you weep, don't you mourn. ___

Oh, Ma – ry, don't you weep, don't you mourn. ___

Phar – aoh's ar – my got drown – ed;

oh, Ma – ry, don't you weep.

Oh, Mary, Don't You Weep

American Spiritual

Chorus: *Oh, Mary, don't you weep, don't you mourn.*
Oh, Mary, don't you weep, don't you mourn.
Pharaoh's army got drowned;
Oh, Mary, don't you weep.

If I could I surely would,
Stand on the rock where Moses stood.
Pharaoh's army got drowned;
Oh, Mary, don't you weep.

Wonder what Satan's been grumblin' 'bout,
Chained in hell so's he can't git out.
Pharaoh's army got drowned;
Oh, Mary, don't you weep.

Chorus

Ol' Satan's crazed an' I am glad,
Missed that soul he thought he had.
Pharaoh's army got drowned;
Oh, Mary, don't you weep.

Took me on down to the valley to pray,
My soul got happy and stayed all day.
Pharaoh's army got drowned;
Oh, Mary, don't you weep.

Chorus

Mary wore three links of chain;
Ev'ry link bore Jesus' name.
Pharaoh's army got drowned;
Oh, Mary, don't you weep.

Scale of G Major

Scale of G Major

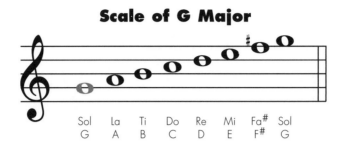

Sol	La	Ti	Do	Re	Mi	Fa#	Sol
G	A	B	C	D	E	F#	G

Fingerboard

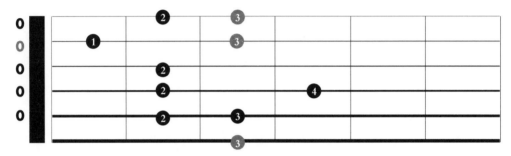

Fingering positions of scale extending over two octaves, beginning on the third fret.

Scale of E Melodic Minor

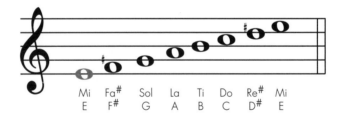

Mi	Fa#	Sol	La	Ti	Do	Re#	Mi
E	F#	G	A	B	C	D#	E

Fingerboard

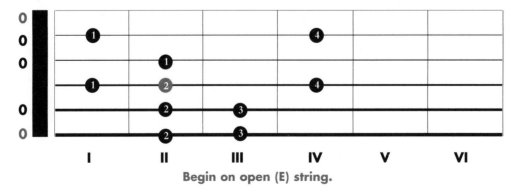

Begin on open (E) string.

Chord Diagrams for "The Water Is Wide"

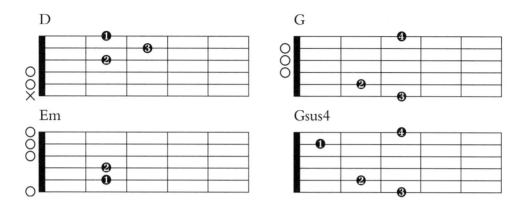

Rhythm Chart for "The Water Is Wide"

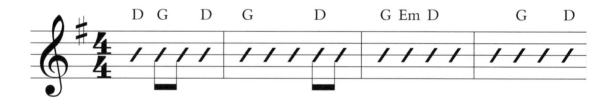

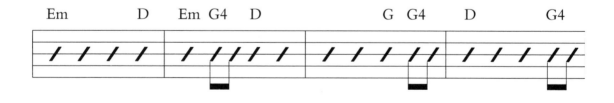

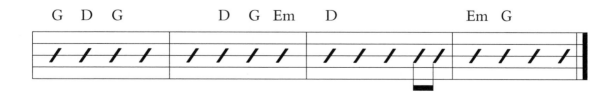

The Water Is Wide

American folk song

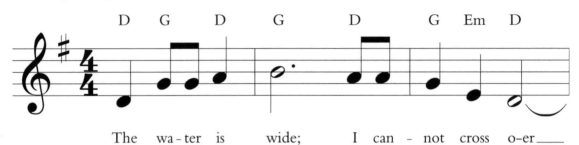

The wa-ter is wide; I can-not cross o-er____

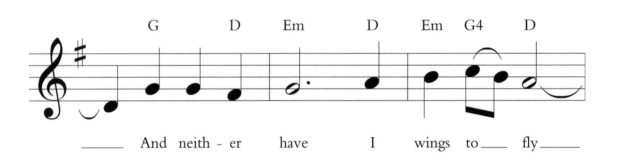

____ And neith-er have I wings to ___ fly____

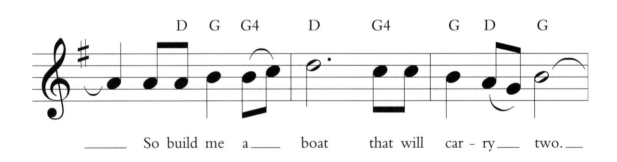

____ So build me a____ boat that will car-ry___ two.____

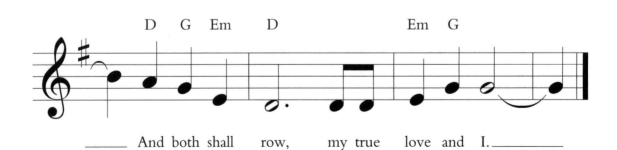

____ And both shall row, my true love and I.____

The Water Is Wide

American Folk Song

The water is wide; I cannot cross o'er.
And neither have I wings to fly.
So build me a boat that will carry two,
And both shall row, my true love and I.

A ship there is and she sails the sea.
She's loaded deep as deep can be.
But not so deep as the love I'm in;
I know not if I sink or swim.

I leaned my back against an oak,
For thought it I a trusty tree,
But first it bent and then it broke.
Thus did my love prove false to me.

I reached my finger 'neath a rose,
Hoping the fairest flower to find.
I pricked my finger to the bone
And left the fairest bloom behind.

Oh, love be handsome and love be kind,
Bright as a jewel whose sheen is new.
But love grows old and waxes cold,
And fades away like the morning dew.

Must I go bound while you go free,
Must I love one who does not love me,
Must I be born with so little art,
As to love a man who'll break my heart?

When cockle shells turn silver bells,
Then will my love come back to me,
When roses bloom in winter's gloom,
Then will my love return to me.

Lyrics for "The Water Is Wide" have multiple versions and variations; the traditional song dates at least from the 18th century in America. Some have claimed Scottish and others Irish origin; it was widespread in Britain. In 1724, an early version of the song was published as "O Waly, Waly," and in 1776 the ballad "Lord Jamie Douglas," a longer version, was published. The point of view, depending on the lyrics, can of course be male or female. The earliest versions refer to a false maid and a broken-hearted male (the singer).

D Major
Scale & Chords

Scale of D Major

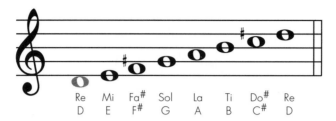

Fingerboard

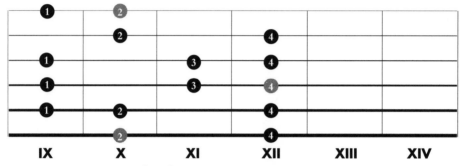

IX   X   XI   XII   XIII   XIV

Fingering positions of scale over two octaves, starting at the tenth fret.

Scale of B Minor

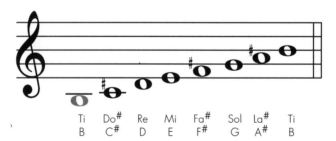

Fingerboard

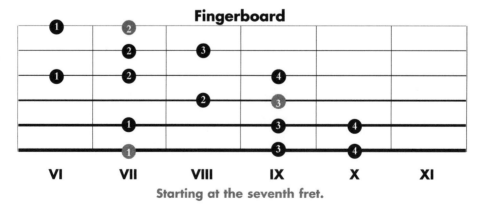

VI   VII   VIII   IX   X   XI

Starting at the seventh fret.

Barré Chords

Let's use the song "Spanish Is the Loving Tongue" for a study in the use of barré chords. Remember that barré chords are formed by placing the forefinger of the left hand across some of the strings. This forms a temporary nut.

Barré Chord Diagrams for "Spanish Is the Loving Tongue"

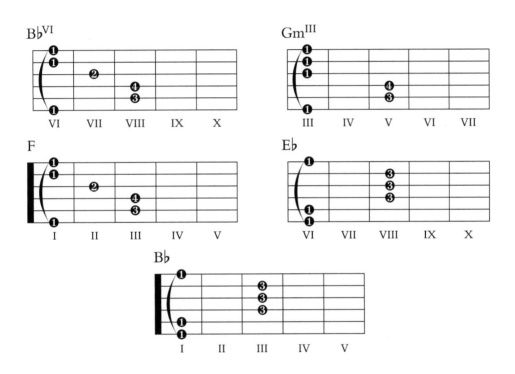

Rhythm Chart for "Spanish Is the Loving Tongue"

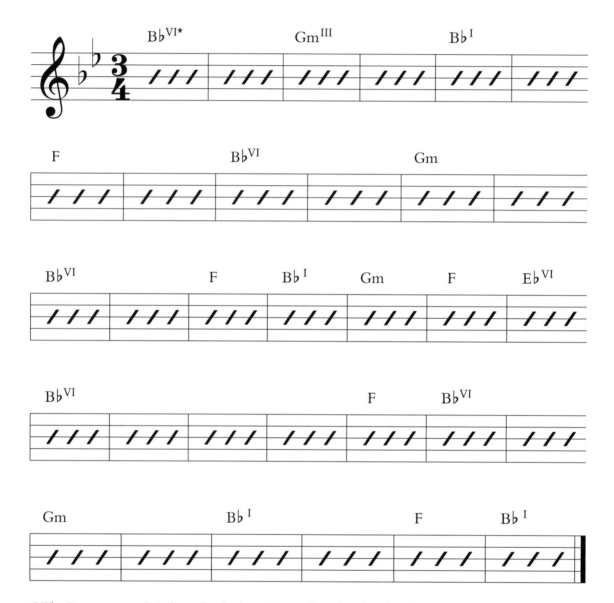

The Roman numerals indicate the chord position on the guitar fingerboard.

Spanish Is the Loving Tongue

American cowboy ballad   *Charles Badger Clark, Jr.*

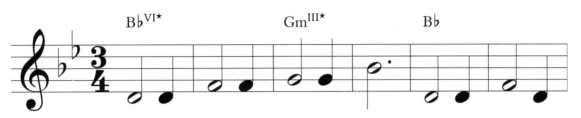

Span-ish   is   the   lov - ing   tongue,   soft   as   mu - sic,

light   as   spray.   'Twas a   girl I   learned it   from,   liv - ing

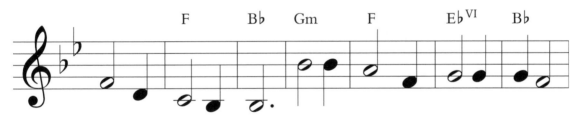

down So - nor - a   way.   I don't look much like a   lov - er,

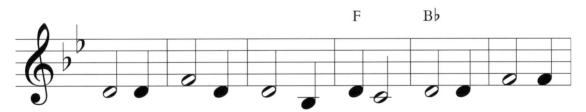

Yet   I   say   her   love words   o - ver,   oft - en   when I'm

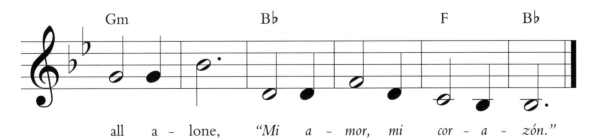

all   a - lone,   "*Mi   a - mor, mi   cor - a - zón.*"

★ *indicates chord position*

Spanish Is the Loving Tongue

Charles Badger Clark, Jr.

American Cowboy Ballad

Spanish is the loving tongue,
Soft as music, light as spray.
'Twas a girl I learned it from,
Living down Sonora way.
I don't look much like a lover,
Yet I say her love words over,
Often when I'm all alone,
"Mi amor, mi corazón."

Nights when she knew that I'd ride,
She would listen for my spurs,
Throw the big door open wide,
Raise them laughin' eyes of hers.
How my heart would nigh stop beating
When I'd hear her tender greeting,
Whispered soft for me alone—
"Mi amor, mi corazón."

Moonlight on the patio,
Old señora nodding near,
Me and Juana talking low,
So the *madre* couldn't hear.
How those hours would go a-flyin'
And too soon I'd hear her sighing
In that little sorry tone—
"Mi amor, mi corazón."

Never seen her since that night,
I can't cross the line, you know.
Wanted for a gamblin' fight,
Maybe it's just better so.
Yet I've always sort of missed her
Since that last sad night I kissed her;
Left her heart and lost my own,
"Adiós, mi corazón."

Key of A Major Scales & Chords

Scale of A Major

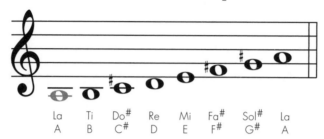

La	Ti	Do#	Re	Mi	Fa#	Sol#	La
A	B	C#	D	E	F#	G#	A

Fingerboard

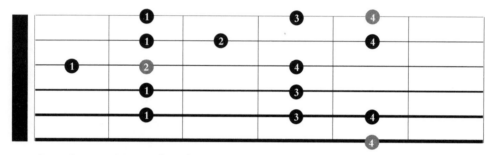

Fingering positions of scale over two octaves, starting at the fifth fret.

Scale of F# Minor

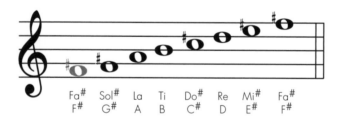

Fa#	Sol#	La	Ti	Do#	Re	Mi#	Fa#
F#	G#	A	B	C#	D	E#	F#

Fingerboard

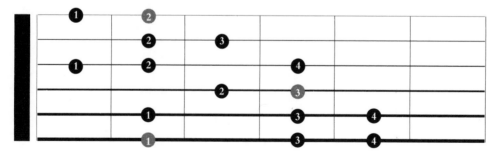

Starting on the second fret. (This is one octave below that notated on the staff.)

Chords Diagrams for "My Country, 'Tis of Thee"

C
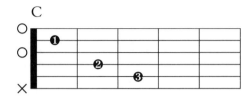

G
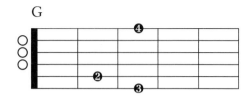

F
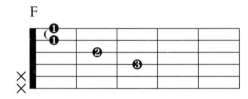

Am
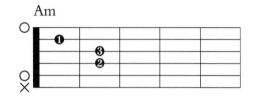

G7
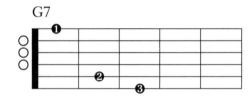

Cadd5
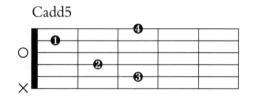

F^{V}
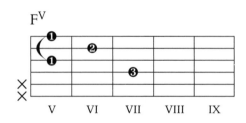

Rhythm Chart for "My Country, 'Tis of Thee"

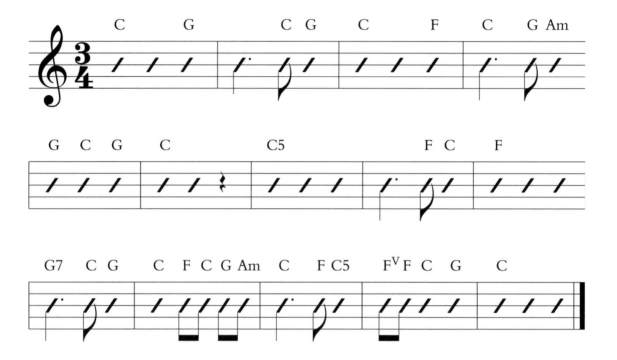

Watch out for the dotted quarter and eighth notes.

This anthem, "My Country, 'Tis of Thee," still called "God Save the King" and sung with different lyrics in Great Britain, was altered in the United States after the American Revolution. Play it in a stately manner, rather slowly.

My Country, 'Tis of Thee

British and American anthem

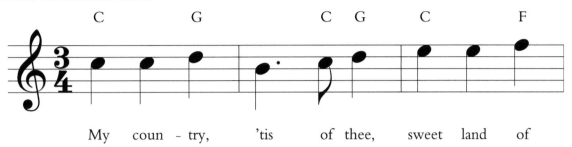

My coun - try,   'tis   of thee,   sweet land of

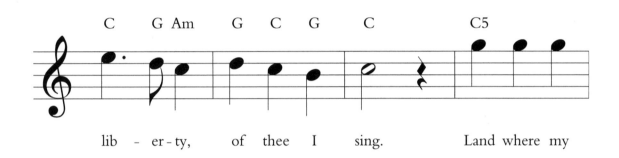

lib - er - ty,   of thee I   sing.   Land where my

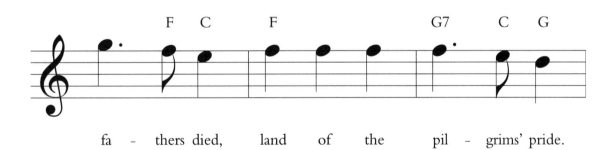

fa - thers died,   land   of   the   pil - grims' pride.

From ev - er - y moun - tain-side,   let __ free - dom   ring.

My Country, 'Tis of Thee

British and American Anthem

My country, 'tis of thee,
Sweet land of liberty,
Of thee I sing;
Land where my fathers died,
Land of the pilgrims' pride,
From every mountainside,
Let freedom ring.

My native country, thee,
Land of the noble free,
Thy name I love;
I love thy rocks and rills,
Thy woods and templed hills;
My heart with rapture thrills
Like that above.

Let music swell the breeze,
And ring from all the trees
Sweet freedom's song;
Let mortal tongues awake,
Let all that breathe partake,
Let rocks their silence break,
The sound prolong.

Our fathers' God, to thee,
Author of liberty,
To Thee we sing:
Long may our land be bright
With freedom's holy light;
Protect us with Thy might,
Great God, our King.

Key of E Major
Scales & Chords

Scale of E Major

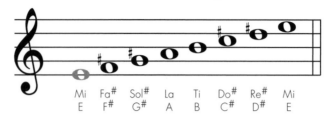

Mi	Fa#	Sol#	La	Ti	Do#	Re#	Mi
E	F#	G#	A	B	C#	D#	E

Fingerboard

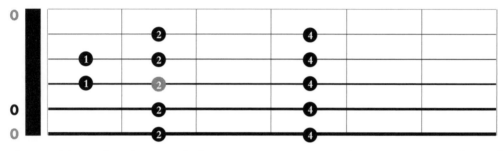

Fingering positions of scale extended over two octaves, starting on open (E) string. (This is one octave below that notated on the staff.)

Scale of C# Minor

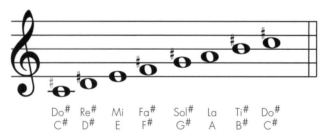

Do#	Re#	Mi	Fa#	Sol#	La	Ti#	Do#
C#	D#	E	F#	G#	A	B#	C#

Fingerboard

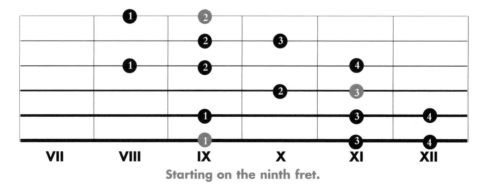

Starting on the ninth fret.

Chord Diagrams for "Drink to Me Only with Thine Eyes"

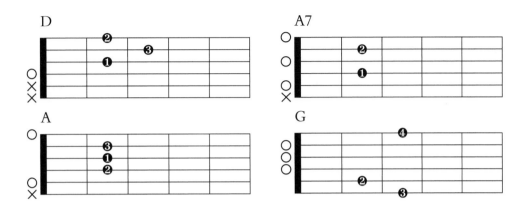

Rhythm Chart for "Drink to Me Only with Thine Eyes"

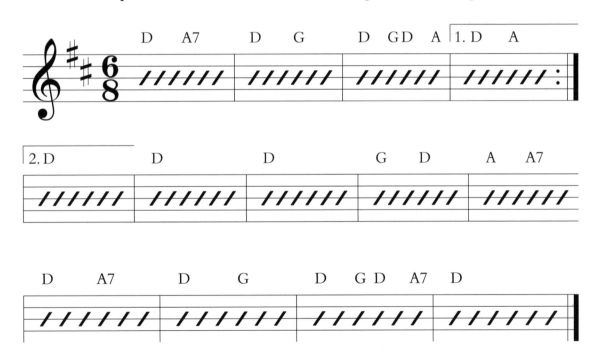

Drink to Me Only with Thine Eyes

Somewhat slowly

Ben Jonson

Drink to me on - ly   with ___ thine eyes. ___ And
Or leave a kiss   but   in ___ the cup, ___ and

I ___ will pledge with   mine. ___   wine. ___ The
I'll ___ not look for

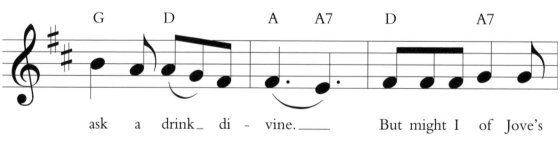

thirst ___ that from   the   soul ___ doth rise   doth

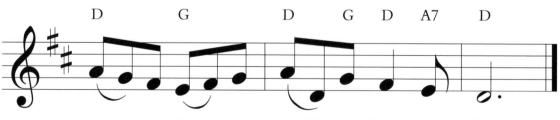

ask a drink _ di - vine. ___   But might I of Jove's

nec - tar sip ___ I would _ not change for   thine.

Drink to Me Only with Thine Eyes
Ben Jonson

Drink to me only with thine eyes,
And I will pledge with mine;
Or leave a kiss but in the cup,
And I'll not ask for wine.
The thirst that from the soul doth rise,
Doth ask a drink divine;
But might I of Jove's nectar sip,
I would not change for thine.

I sent thee late, a rosy wreath,
Not so much honoring thee,
As giving it a hope that there
It could not withered be;
But thou thereon didst only breathe,
And sent it back to me,
Since when it grows and smells, I swear,
Not of itself, but thee!

Key of B
Scales & Chords

Scale of B Major

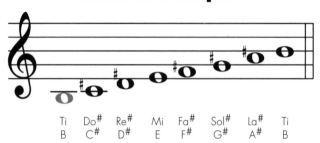

Ti	Do#	Re#	Mi	Fa#	Sol#	La#	Ti
B	C#	D#	E	F#	G#	A#	B

Fingerboard

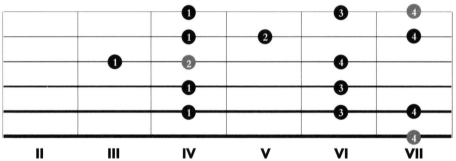

Fingering of scale extended over two octaves, starting on seventh fret.

Scale of G# Minor

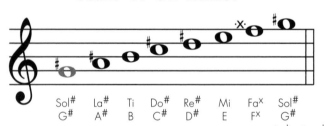

Sol#	La#	Ti	Do#	Re#	Mi	Fa×	Sol#
G#	A#	B	C#	D#	E	F×	G#

•×• indicates double-sharp

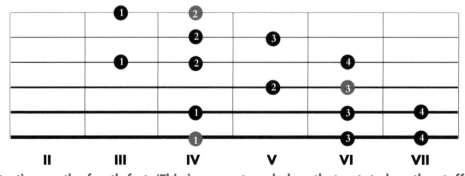

Starting on the fourth fret. (This is one octave below that notated on the staff.)

Chord Diagrams for "Greensleeves"

Em
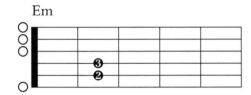

D
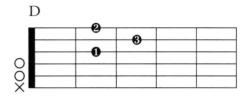

G
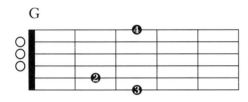

Bm
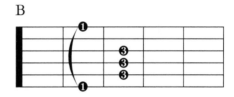

B7
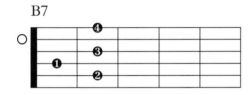

B
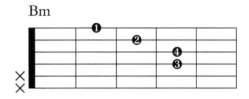

Rhythm Chart for "Greensleeves"

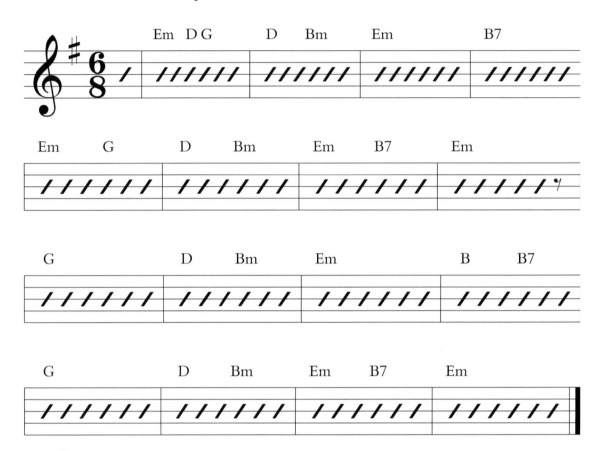

King Henry VIII has been credited with writing the melody, if not the words, to "Greensleeves." We cannot be sure of its origin, but the song is lovely. Play it at a moderate tempo.

Greensleeves

Liltingly

English

Greensleeves
English

Alas my love, you do me wrong
To cast me off discourteously,
For I have loved thee
Oh so long, delighting in your company.

Refrain: Greensleeves was all my joy,
Greensleeves was my delight,
Greensleeves was my heart of gold.
Aye, who but my Lady Greensleeves.

I have been ready at your hand
To grant whatever you would crave,
I have both wagered life and land,
Your love and good will for to have.

Refrain

I bought thee kerchiefs for thy head
That were wrought fine and gallantly,
I kept thee both at board and bed,
Which cost my purse well favoredly.

Refrain

I bought thee petticoats of the best,
The cloth no finer could there be,
I gave thee jewels for thy chest,
And all this cost I spent on thee.

Refrain

Now shall I pray to God on high
That thou my constancy mayst see
And that yet once before I die,
Thou wilt vouchsafe to love me.

Greensleeves, now farewell! Adieu!
God I pray to prosper thee.
For I am still thy lover true,
Come once again and love me.

Key of F Major Scales & Chords

Scale of F major

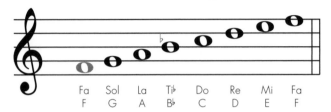

Fa	Sol	La	Ti♭	Do	Re	Mi	Fa
F	G	A	B♭	C	D	E	F

Fingerboard

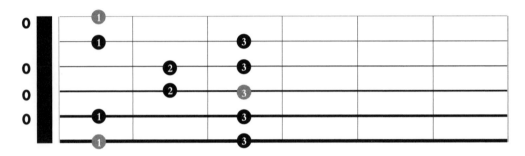

Fingering of scale extended over two octaves, starting on the first fret. (This is one octave below that notated on the staff.)

Scale of D Minor

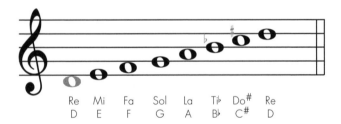

Re	Mi	Fa	Sol	La	Ti♭	Do#	Re
D	E	F	G	A	B♭	C#	D

Fingerboard

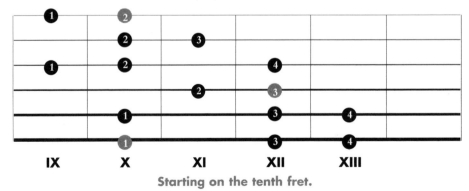

IX   X   XI   XII   XIII

Starting on the tenth fret.

Chord Diagrams for "House of the Rising Sun"

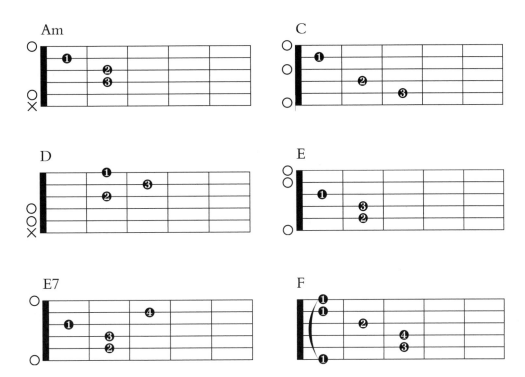

Note: To accomodate the female voice, put a capo on the second or third fret.

Rhythm Chart for "House of the Rising Sun"

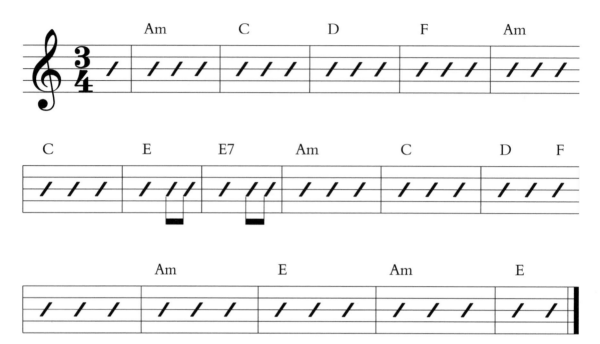

A staple of American folk tradition, "House of the Rising Sun," is usually heard played in arpeggio style (see Chapter 6 for detailed instruction).

House of the Rising Sun

American blues ballad

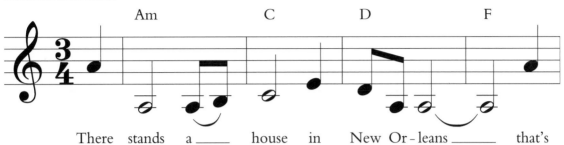

There stands a ____ house in New Or-leans ____ that's

called the Ri - sing ____ sun. _____ It has

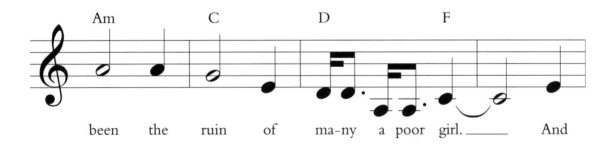

been the ruin of ma-ny a poor girl. ____ And

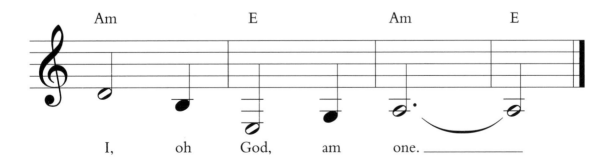

I, oh God, am one. _____

House of the Rising Sun

American Blues Ballad

There stands a house in New Orleans
That's called the Rising Sun.
It has been the ruin of many a poor girl
And I, oh, God, am one.

My mama was a tailor,
She sewed them old blue jeans;
My daddy was a gamblin' man
Down in New Orleans.

My husband was a Jack of Knaves
Played cards in every town,
And the only time he was satisfied
Was when he drunk his liquor down.

Now the only thing a gambler needs
Is a suitcase and a trunk;
And the only time he's satisfied
Is when he's on a drunk.

Go tell my baby sister
Not to do what I have done.
Just walk past that house in New Orleans
They call the Rising Sun.

Now one foot's on the platform,
The other's on the train
I'm goin' back to New Orleans
To wear that ball and chain.

I'm going back to New Orleans
My race is almost run;
I'm going back to pass my life
Beneath the Rising Sun.

Key of B♭ Major Scales & Chords

Scale of B♭ Major

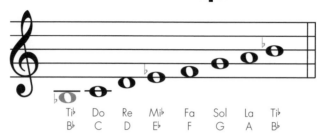

Ti♭	Do	Re	Mi♭	Fa	Sol	La	Ti♭
B♭	C	D	E♭	F	G	A	B♭

Fingerboard

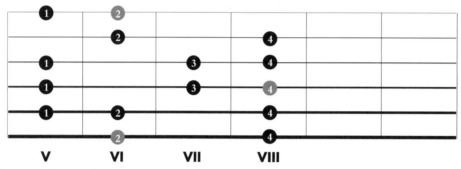

Fingering positions of the scale extended over two octaves, starting on the second fret.

Scale of G Minor

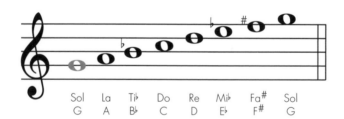

Sol	La	Ti♭	Do	Re	Mi♭	Fa#	Sol
G	A	B♭	C	D	E♭	F#	G

Fingerboard

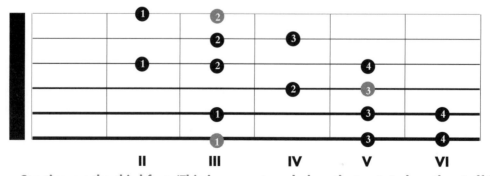

Starting on the third fret. (This is one octave below that notated on the staff.)

Chord Diagrams for "The Ash Grove"

F
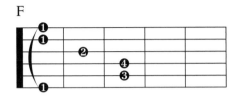

Gm
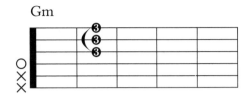

G7
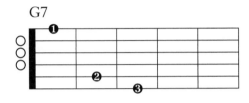

C
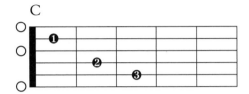

B♭
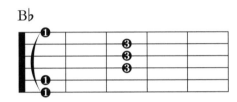

C7
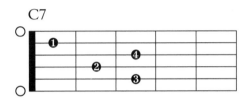

D7
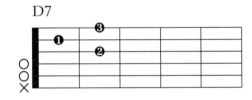

Dm
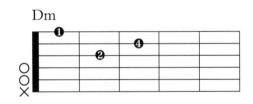

Rhythm Chart for "The Ash Grove"

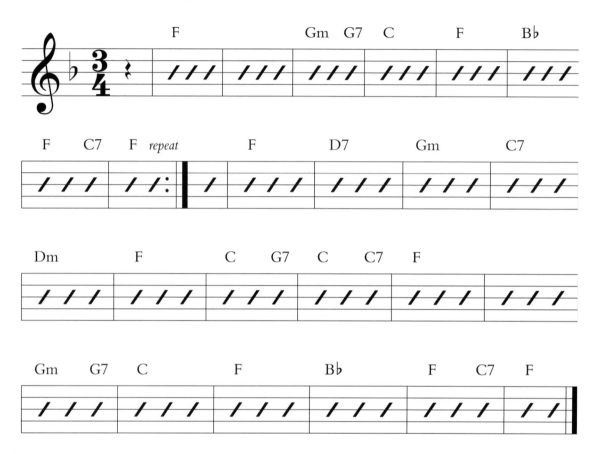

The lovely melody of "The Ash Grove," a perennial folk favorite, is also heard (with different lyrics, of course) in the Welsh national anthem. It should be played at a lively tempo. If you find the key too low for your voice, try putting a capo on the second fret. (If you did that, in what key would you then be playing?)

The Ash Grove

Welsh

1. Down yon-der green__ val-ley where stream-lets__ me-
2. Or at the bright__ noon-tide in sol - i - tude__

an-der, when twi-light_ is ___ fad-ing, I pen-sive-ly roam.
wan-der, a - mid the_ dark_ shades of the lone-ly ash grove.

'Twas__ there while_ the ___ black-bird was cheer-ful - ly ___

sing-ing, I first met_ that__ dear one, the joy of my

heart. A - round us for__ glad-ness the blue-bells_ were_

ring-ing. Ah! Then lit - tle__ thought I how soon we should part.

The Ash Grove

Welsh

Down yonder green valley, where streamlets meander,
When twilight is fading, I pensively roam.
Or at the bright noontide in solitude wander,
Amid the dark shades of the lonely ash grove.
'Twas there while the blackbird was cheerfully singing,
I first met that dear one, the joy of my heart;
Around us for gladness the bluebells were ringing,
Ah! Then little thought I how soon we should part.

Still glows the bright sunshine o'er valley and mountain,
Still warbles the blackbird its note from the tree;
Still trembles the moonbeam on streamlet and fountain,
But what are the beauties of nature to me?
With sorrow, deep sorrow, my bosom is laden,
All day I go mourning in search of my love.
Ye echoes! Oh, tell me, where is the sweet maiden?
"She sleeps 'neath the green turf, down by the ash grove."

Key of E♭ Major Scales & Chords

Scale of E♭ Major

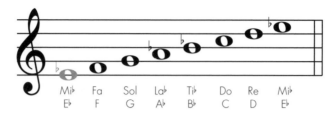

Mi♭	Fa	Sol	La♭	Ti♭	Do	Re	Mi♭
E♭	F	G	A♭	B♭	C	D	E♭

Fingerboard

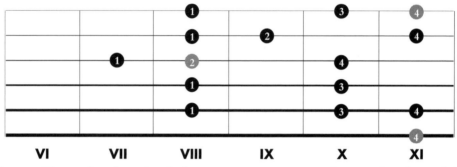

Fingering positions of scale extended over two octaves, starting on the eleventh fret.

Scale of C Minor

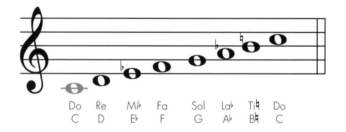

Do	Re	Mi♭	Fa	Sol	La♭	Ti♮	Do
C	D	E♭	F	G	A♭	B♮	C

Fingerboard

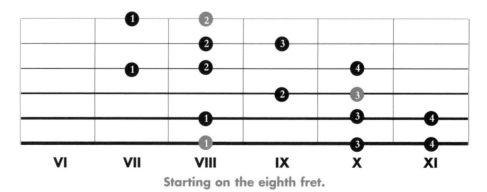

Starting on the eighth fret.

Chord Diagrams for "All Through the Night"

G
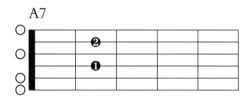

Em
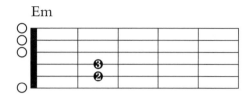

A7
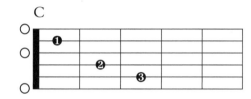

D
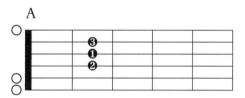

C
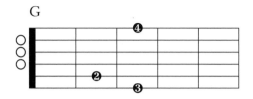

A
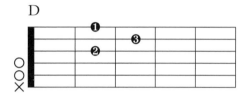

Am
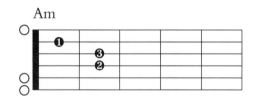

Rhythm Chart for "All Through the Night"

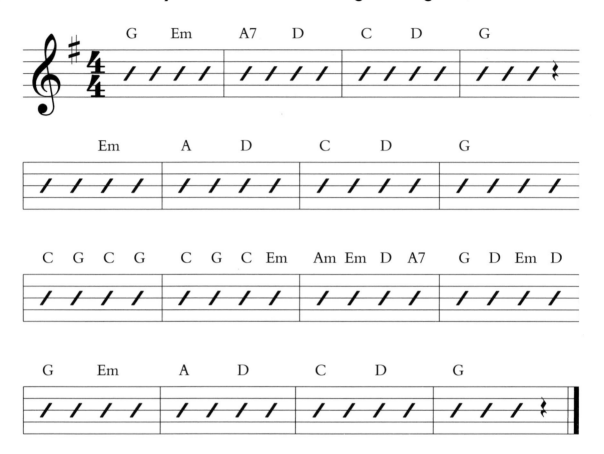

This poetic lullaby should be played squarely and slowly to match the cadence of the words. Since there are several chords to learn following quickly one upon the other, practice the sequence several times before attempting to perform the song itself.

All Through the Night

Welsh lullaby

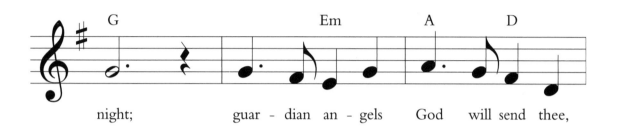

Sleep, my love, and peace at - tend thee, all through the

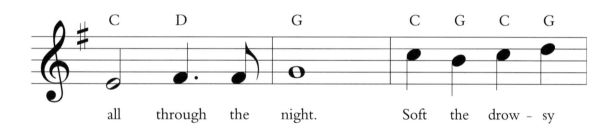

night; guar - dian an - gels God will send thee,

all through the night. Soft the drow - sy

hours are creep-ing, hill and vale in slum - ber steep-ing;

love a - lone his watch is keep-ing, all through the night.

All Through the Night

Welsh Lullaby

Sleep, my love, and peace attend thee,
All through the night;
Guardian angels God will send thee,
All through the night.
Soft the drowsy hours are creeping,
Hill and vale in slumber sleeping;
Love alone his watch is keeping,
All through the night.

Though I roam a minstrel lonely,
All through the night;
My true harp shall praise thee only,
All through the night.
Love's young dream, alas, is over,
Yet my strains of love shall hover,
Near the presence of my lover,
All through the night.

Hark! A solemn bell is ringing,
Clear through the night;
Thou, my love, art heavenward winging,
Home through the night.
Earthly dust from off thee shaken,
Soul immortal thou shalt waken,
With thy last dim journey taken,
Home through the night.

Key of A♭ Major
Scales & Chords

Scale of A♭ Major

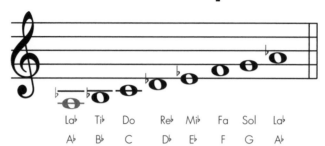

Lab	Tib	Do	Reb	Mib	Fa	Sol	Lab
A♭	B♭	C	D♭	E♭	F	G	A♭

Fingerboard

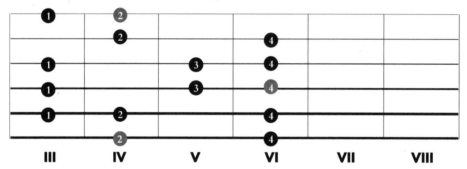

Fingering position of scale extended over two octaves, starting on second fret.

Scale of F Minor

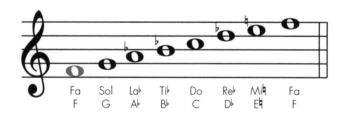

Fa	Sol	Lab	Tib	Do	Reb	Mi♮	Fa
F	G	A♭	B♭	C	D♭	E♮	F

Fingerboard

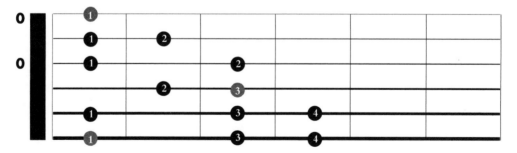

Starting on the first fret. (This is one octave below that notated on the staff.)

Chord Diagrams for "Scarborough Fair"

Dm
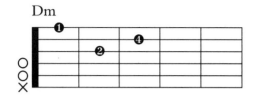

Am
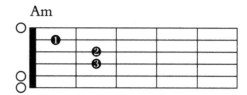

C
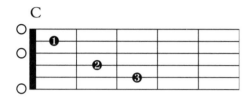

F
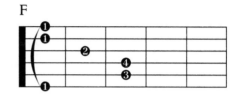

G
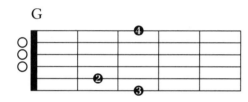

Am7
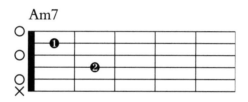

Rhythm Chart for "Scarborough Fair"

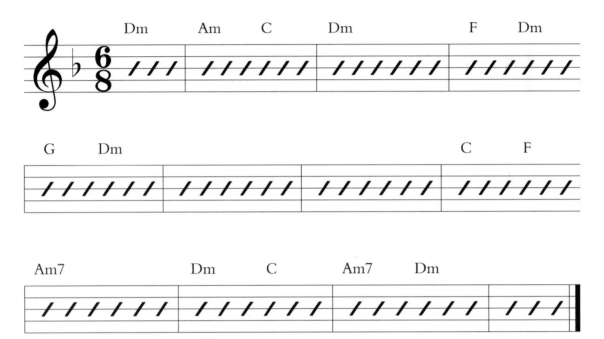

For this traditional English ballad, made famous by Simon and Garfunkel's exquisite recording, a finger-picking style of accompaniment would be most appropriate. After strumming through the chord progression until the changes are smooth, try working out a two- or three-finger picking pattern, alternating the low strings (using the thumb) with the three high ones (using the first and second fingers).

Scarborough Fair

English ballad
Lightly

Are you go - ing to Scar - bor - ough Fair?

Parse - ly, sage, rose - mar - y, and thyme.

Re - mem - ber me to the one who lives there. For

she was once a true love of mine.

Scarborough Fair

English Ballad

Are you going to Scarborough Fair?
Parsley, sage, rosemary, and thyme.
Remember me to the one who lives there,
For she was once a true love of mine.

Greet her who made me a cambric shirt,
Parsley, sage, rosemary, and thyme,
Without false seam or fine needle work,
For she was once a true love of mine.

Tell her to wash it in yonder dry well,
Parsley, sage, rosemary, and thyme,
Where water ne'er sprang nor drop of rain fell,
She who was once a true love of mine.

Tell her to dry it on yonder thorn,
Parsley, sage, rosemary, and thyme,
Which never bore blossom since Adam was born,
For she was once a true love of mine.

And tell her to find me an acre of land,
Parsley, sage, rosemary, and thyme,
Between the sea foam and the sea sand,
For she was once a true love of mine.

Then might you plow it with a lamb's horn,
Parsley, sage, rosemary, and thyme,
And sow the whole field with one peppercorn,
For she was once a true love of mine.

Then canst thou reap it with sickle of leather,
Parsley, sage, rosemary, and thyme,
And tie it all up with a blue peacock feather,
For she was once a true love of mine.

And when you have done and finished your work,
Parsley, sage, rosemary, and thyme,
Then come and behold her cambric shirt,
For she was once a true love of mine.

Key of D♭ (C♯) Major Scales & Chords

Scale of D♭ (C♯) Major

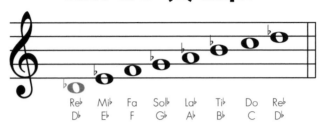

Re♭	Mi♭	Fa	Sol♭	La♭	Ti♭	Do	Re♭
D♭	E♭	F	G♭	A♭	B♭	C	D♭

Fingerboard

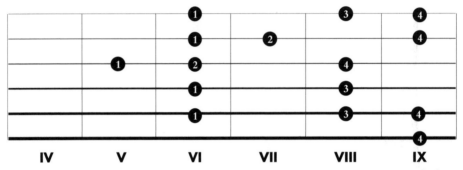

IV	V	VI	VII	VIII	IX

Fingering position of scale extended over two octaves, starting on ninth fret.

Scale of B♭ minor

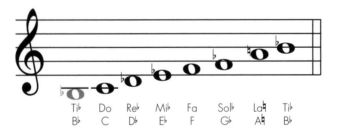

Ti♭	Do	Re♭	Mi♭	Fa	Sol♭	La♮	Ti♭
B♭	C	D♭	E♭	F	G♭	A♮	B♭

Fingerboard

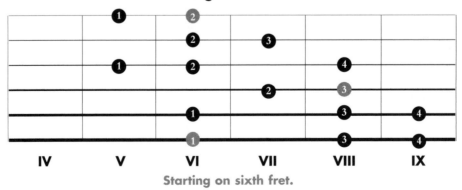

IV	V	VI	VII	VIII	IX

Starting on sixth fret.

Chords Diagrams for "Amazing Grace"

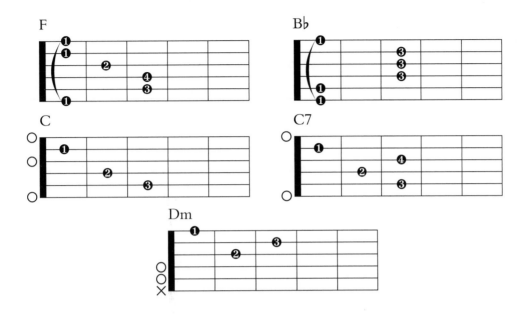

Rhythm Chart for "Amazing Grace"

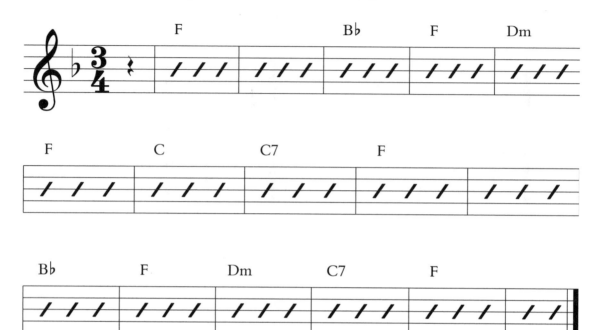

The composer of "Amazing Grace," John Newton (1725-1807), was a slave dealer who repented of his inhumanity and thereafter never plied his nefarious trade again. After a dramatic conversion, he wrote his deeply felt hymn. It should be played rather slowly and solemnly. There have been many versions and variations on his original lyrics. Here's one version.

Amazing Grace

John Newton

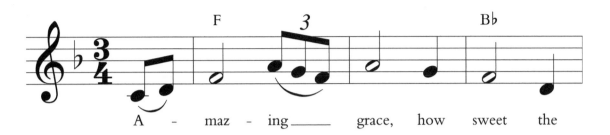

A - maz - ing____ grace, how sweet the

sound that __ saved a _____ wretch like __ me; _____ I ___

once was ____ lost, but now I'm found, was __

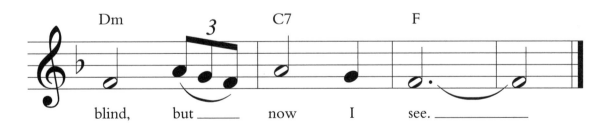

blind, but ____ now I see. _____

Amazing Grace

John Newton

Amazing grace, how sweet the sound
That saved a wretch like me.
I once was lost, but now I'm found,
Was blind, but now I see.

'Twas grace that taught my heart to fear
And grace that fear relieved.
How precious did that grace appear
The hour I first believed.

Through many dangers, toils, and snares,
I have already come.
'Tis grace has brought me safe, thus far,
And grace will lead me home.

The Lord has promised good to me,
His word my hope secures;
He will my shield and portion be,
As long as life endures.

When we've been here ten thousand years
Bright shining as the sun,
We've no less days to sing God's praise
Than when we first begun.

Key of G♭ (F♯) Major Scales & Chords

Scale of G♭ (F♯) Major

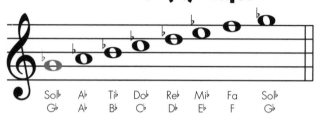

Sol♭	A♭	Ti♭	Do♭	Re♭	Mi♭	Fa	Sol♭
G♭	A♭	B♭	C♭	D♭	E♭	F	G♭

Fingerboard

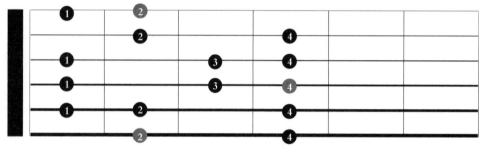

Fingering position of scale extended over two octaves, starting on second fret. (This is one octave below that notated on the staff.)

Scale of E♭ Minor

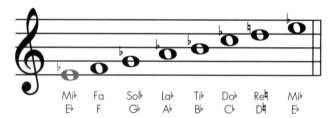

Mi♭	Fa	Sol♭	La♭	Ti♭	Do♭	Re♮	Mi♭
E♭	F	G♭	A♭	B♭	C♭	D♮	E♭

Fingerboard

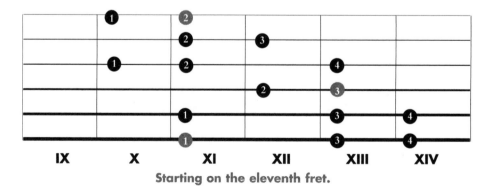

Starting on the eleventh fret.

Chord Diagrams for "Hark! The Herald Angels Sing!"

D
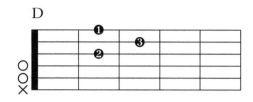

G
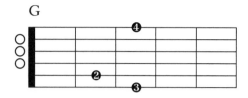

G5
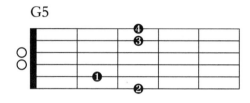

C
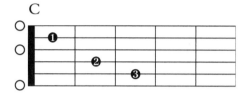

Bm
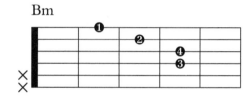

Em
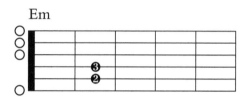

Em
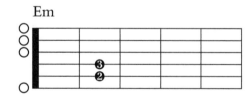

Am
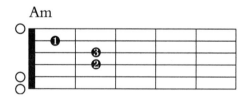

Rhythm Chart for "Hark! The Herald Angels Sing!"

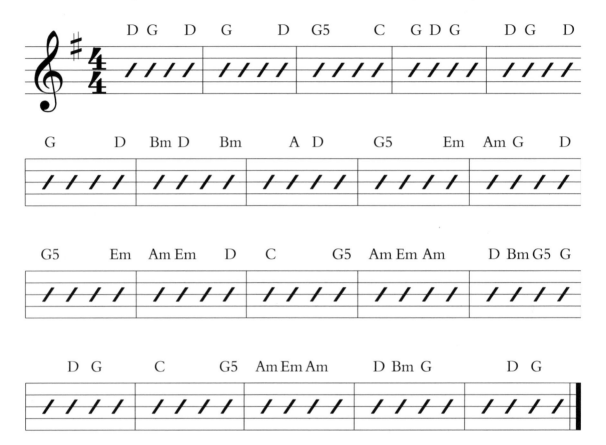

Mastering the swift chord changes needed to play this famous carol requires some concentration, but the end result of such practice is always rewarding. The music was composed by the great Felix Mendelssohn.

Hark! The Herald Angels Sing!

Felix Mendelssohn and Charles Wesley

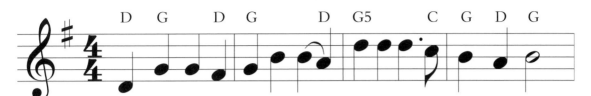

Hark! The her-ald an-gels sing, _ "Glo-ry to the new-born King!"

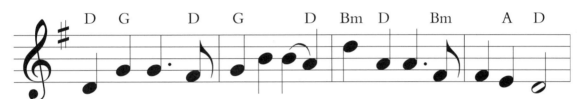

Peace on earth and mer-cy mild, _ God and sin-ners re-con-ciled.

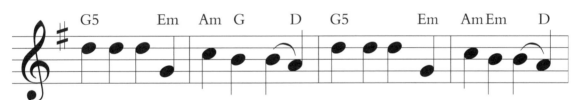

Joy-ful, all ye na-tions, rise. __ Join the tri-umph of the skies; _

with an-gel-ic hosts pro-claim, "Christ is _ born in Beth-le-hem."

Hark! The her-ald an-gels sing, "Glo-ry_ to the new-born King!"

Hark! The Herald Angels Sing

Felix Mendelssohn and Charles Wesley

Hark! The herald angels sing,
"Glory to the newborn King!"
Peace on earth and mercy mild,
God and sinners reconciled.
Joyful, all ye nations, rise,
Join the triumph of the skies;
With angelic hosts proclaim,
"Christ is born in Bethlehem."
Hark! The herald angels sing,
"Glory to the newborn King!"

Christ, by highest heaven adored;
Christ, the everlasting Lord;
Late in time behold him come,
Offspring of the favored one.
Veiled in flesh, the Godhead see:
Hail the incarnate Deity,
Pleased, as man with man to dwell,
Jesus, our Emmanuel!
Hark! The herald angels sing,
"Glory to the newborn King!"

Hail! The heaven-born Prince of Peace!
Hail! The Son of Righteousness!
Light and life to all He brings,
Risen with healing in His wings.
Mild He lays His glory by,
Born that man no more may die;
Born to raise the sons of earth,
Born to give them second birth.
Hark! The herald angels sing,
"Glory to the newborn King!"

Chapter 4

Chord Composition

Augmented Chord

The augmented chord is composed of the tonic, the third, and the augmented fifth.

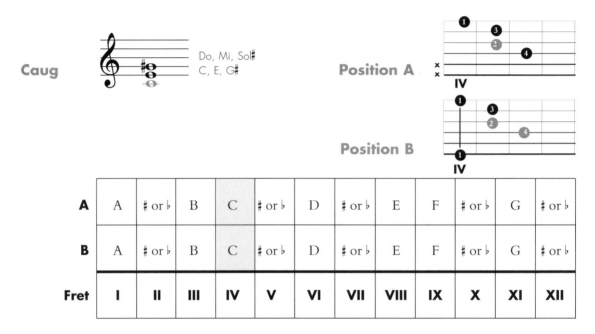

Caug

Do, Mi, Sol#
C, E, G#

Position A

Position B

	I	II	III	IV	V	VI	VII	VIII	IX	X	XI	XII
A	A	# or ♭	B	C	# or ♭	D	# or ♭	E	F	# or ♭	G	# or ♭
B	A	# or ♭	B	C	# or ♭	D	# or ♭	E	F	# or ♭	G	# or ♭
Fret	I	II	III	IV	V	VI	VII	VIII	IX	X	XI	XII

Sixth Chord

The sixth chord is composed of the tonic, the third, the fifth, and the major sixth.

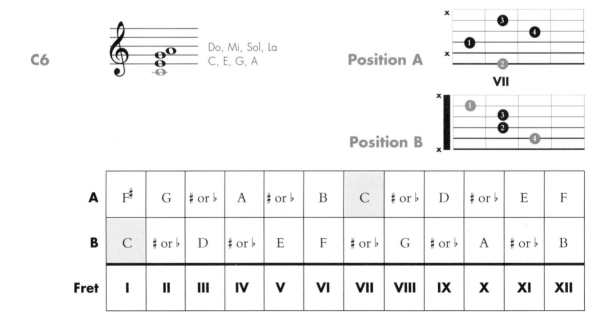

C6

Do, Mi, Sol, La
C, E, G, A

Position A

Position B

	I	II	III	IV	V	VI	VII	VIII	IX	X	XI	XII
A	F#	G	# or ♭	A	# or ♭	B	C	# or ♭	D	# or ♭	E	F
B	C	# or ♭	D	# or ♭	E	F	# or ♭	G	# or ♭	A	# or ♭	B
Fret	I	II	III	IV	V	VI	VII	VIII	IX	X	XI	XII

Minor Sixth Chord

The minor sixth chord is composed of the tonic, the minor third, the fifth, and the sixth.

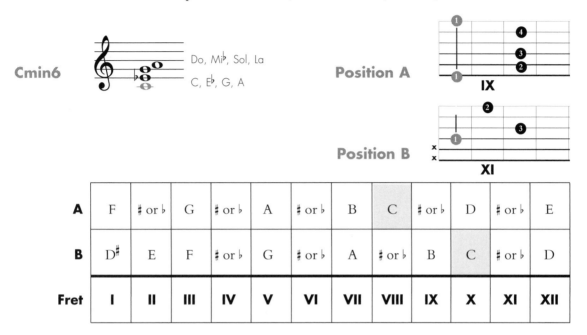

Cmin6   Do, Mi♭, Sol, La
C, E♭, G, A

Position A

Position B

	I		II		III		IV		V		VI		VII	VIII		IX		X		XI		XII
A	F	♯ or ♭	G	♯ or ♭	A	♯ or ♭	B		C	♯ or ♭	D	♯ or ♭	E
B	D♯	E	F	♯ or ♭	G	♯ or ♭	A	♯ or ♭	B		C	♯ or ♭	D
Fret	I	II	III	IV	V	VI	VII	VIII	IX	X	XI	XII	

Added Ninth Chord

The added ninth chord is composed of the tonic, the third, the fifth, the sixth, and the ninth.

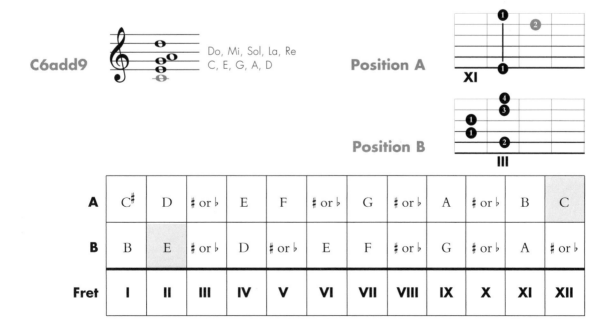

C6add9   Do, Mi, Sol, La, Re
C, E, G, A, D

Position A

Position B

	I		II		III		IV		V		VI		VII	VIII		IX		X		XI		XII
A	C♯	D	♯ or ♭	E	F	♯ or ♭	G	♯ or ♭	A	♯ or ♭	B	C
B	B	E	♯ or ♭	D	♯ or ♭	E	F	♯ or ♭	G	♯ or ♭	A	♯ or ♭
Fret	I	II	III	IV	V	VI	VII	VIII	IX	X	XI	XII	

Dominant Seventh Chord

The dominant seventh chord is composed of the tonic, the major third, the fifth, and the dominant (or minor) seventh.

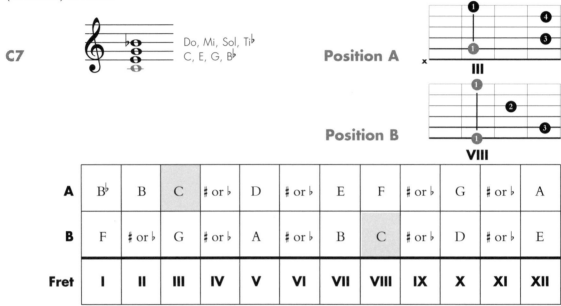

C7

Do, Mi, Sol, Ti♭
C, E, G, B♭

Position A

Position B

	I	II	III	IV	V	VI	VII	VIII	IX	X	XI	XII
A	B♭	B	C	♯ or ♭	D	♯ or ♭	E	F	♯ or ♭	G	♯ or ♭	A
B	F	♯ or ♭	G	♯ or ♭	A	♯ or ♭	B	C	♯ or ♭	D	♯ or ♭	E
Fret	I	II	III	IV	V	VI	VII	VIII	IX	X	XI	XII

Minor Seventh Chord

The minor seventh chord is composed of the tonic, the minor third, the fifth, and the minor (dominant) seventh.

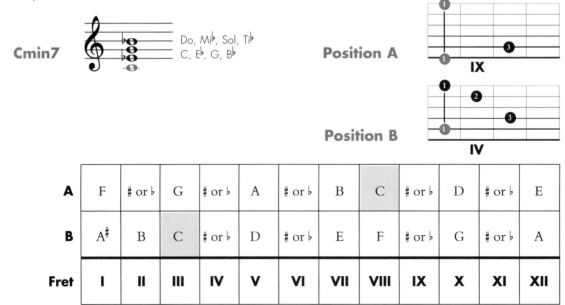

Cmin7

Do, Mi♭, Sol, Ti♭
C, E♭, G, B♭

Position A

Position B

	I	II	III	IV	V	VI	VII	VIII	IX	X	XI	XII
A	F	♯ or ♭	G	♯ or ♭	A	♯ or ♭	B	C	♯ or ♭	D	♯ or ♭	E
B	A♯	B	C	♯ or ♭	D	♯ or ♭	E	F	♯ or ♭	G	♯ or ♭	A
Fret	I	II	III	IV	V	VI	VII	VIII	IX	X	XI	XII

Minor Seventh with Diminished Fifth Chord

The minor seventh diminished fifth chord is composed of the tonic, the minor third, the diminished fifth, and the minor (dominant) seventh.

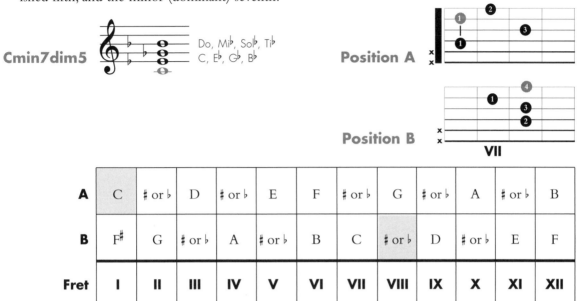

Cmin7dim5

Do, Mi♭, Sol♭, Ti♭
C, E♭, G♭, B♭

Position A

Position B

VII

	I	II	III	IV	V	VI	VII	VIII	IX	X	XI	XII
A	C	♯ or ♭	D	♯ or ♭	E	F	♯ or ♭	G	♯ or ♭	A	♯ or ♭	B
B	F♯	G	♯ or ♭	A	♯ or ♭	B	C	♯ or ♭	D	♯ or ♭	E	F
Fret	I	II	III	IV	V	VI	VII	VIII	IX	X	XI	XII

Major Seventh Chord

The major seventh chord is composed of the tonic, the third, the fifth, and the major seventh.

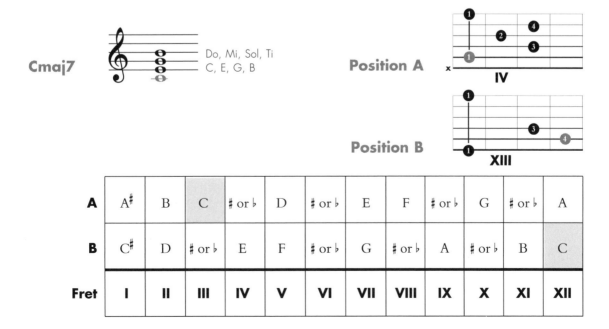

Cmaj7

Do, Mi, Sol, Ti
C, E, G, B

Position A

IV

Position B

XIII

	I	II	III	IV	V	VI	VII	VIII	IX	X	XI	XII
A	A♯	B	C	♯ or ♭	D	♯ or ♭	E	F	♯ or ♭	G	♯ or ♭	A
B	C♯	D	♯ or ♭	E	F	♯ or ♭	G	♯ or ♭	A	♯ or ♭	B	C
Fret	I	II	III	IV	V	VI	VII	VIII	IX	X	XI	XII

Diminished Seventh Chord

The diminished seventh chord is composed of the tonic, the minor third, the diminished fifth, and the diminished seventh.

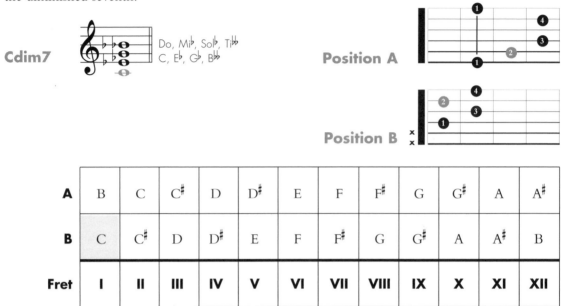

Cdim7 — Do, Mi♭, Sol♭, Ti♭♭ / C, E♭, G♭, B♭♭

Position A

Position B

A	B	C	C#	D	D#	E	F	F#	G	G#	A	A#
B	C	C#	D	D#	E	F	F#	G	G#	A	A#	B
Fret	I	II	III	IV	V	VI	VII	VIII	IX	X	XI	XII

The Minor/Major Seventh Chord

The Minor/Major Seventh Chord is composed of the tonic, the minor third, the fifth, and the major seventh.

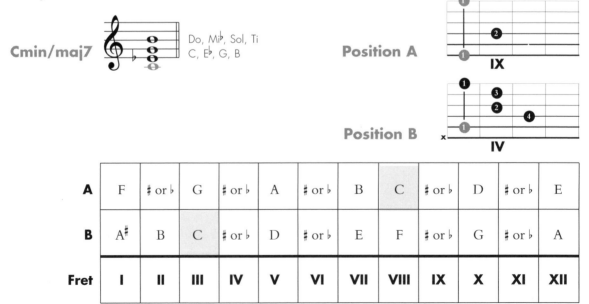

Cmin/maj7 — Do, Mi♭, Sol, Ti / C, E♭, G, B

Position A — IX

Position B — IV

A	F	# or ♭	G	# or ♭	A	# or ♭	B	C	# or ♭	D	# or ♭	E
B	A#	B	C	# or ♭	D	# or ♭	E	F	# or ♭	G	# or ♭	A
Fret	I	II	III	IV	V	VI	VII	VIII	IX	X	XI	XII

Diminished Fifth Minor Seventh Chord

The diminished fifth minor seventh chord is composed of the tonic, the third, the diminished fifth, and the minor seventh.

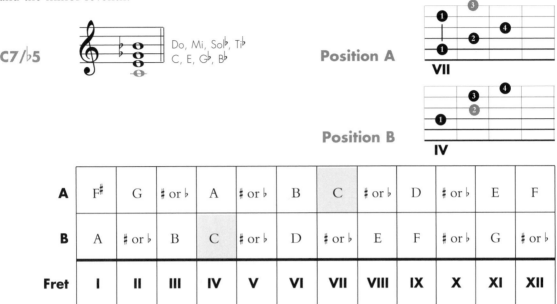

C7/♭5

Do, Mi, Sol♭, Ti♭
C, E, G♭, B♭

Position A

VII

Position B

IV

A	F#	G	# or ♭	A	# or ♭	B	C	# or ♭	D	# or ♭	E	F
B	A	# or ♭	B	C	# or ♭	D	# or ♭	E	F	# or ♭	G	# or ♭
Fret	I	II	III	IV	V	VI	VII	VIII	IX	X	XI	XII

Dominant Seventh Suspended Fourth Chord

The dominant seventh suspended fourth chord is composed of the tonic, the fourth, the fifth, and the minor seventh.

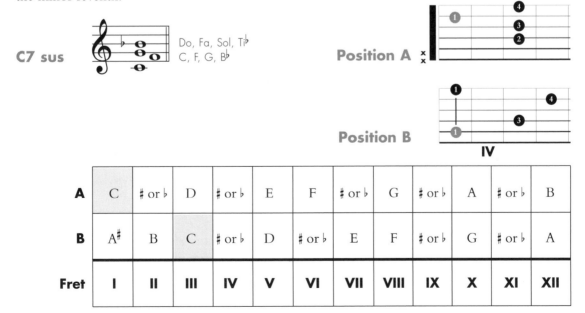

C7 sus

Do, Fa, Sol, Ti♭
C, F, G, B♭

Position A x x

Position B

IV

A	C	# or ♭	D	# or ♭	E	F	# or ♭	G	# or ♭	A	# or ♭	B
B	A#	B	C	# or ♭	D	# or ♭	E	F	# or ♭	G	# or ♭	A
Fret	I	II	III	IV	V	VI	VII	VIII	IX	X	XI	XII

Seventh Add Sixth Chord

The seventh and sixth chord is composed of the tonic, the third, the fifth, the sixth, and the minor seventh.

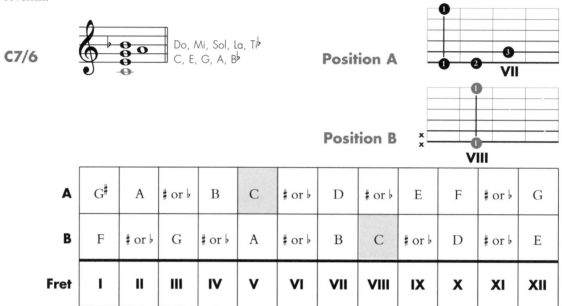

C7/6 — Do, Mi, Sol, La, Ti♭ / C, E, G, A, B♭

Position A — VII

Position B — VIII

	I	II	III	IV	V	VI	VII	VIII	IX	X	XI	XII
A	G♯	A	♯ or ♭	B	C	♯ or ♭	D	♯ or ♭	E	F	♯ or ♭	G
B	F	♯ or ♭	G	♯ or ♭	A	♯ or ♭	B	C	♯ or ♭	D	♯ or ♭	E
Fret	I	II	III	IV	V	VI	VII	VIII	IX	X	XI	XII

Ninth Chord

The ninth chord is composed of the tonic, the third, the fifth, the minor seventh, and the ninth.

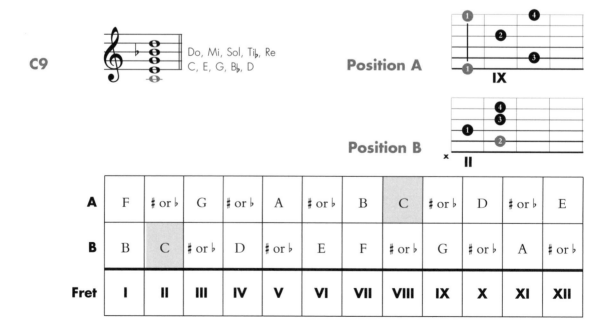

C9 — Do, Mi, Sol, Ti♭, Re / C, E, G, B♭, D

Position A — IX

Position B — II

	I	II	III	IV	V	VI	VII	VIII	IX	X	XI	XII
A	F	♯ or ♭	G	♯ or ♭	A	♯ or ♭	B	C	♯ or ♭	D	♯ or ♭	E
B	B	C	♯ or ♭	D	♯ or ♭	E	F	♯ or ♭	G	♯ or ♭	A	♯ or ♭
Fret	I	II	III	IV	V	VI	VII	VIII	IX	X	XI	XII

Minor Ninth Chord

The minor ninth chord is composed of the tonic, the third, the fifth, the minor seventh, and the ninth.

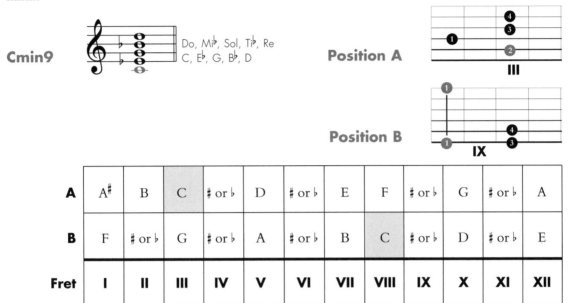

Cmin9

Do, Mi♭, Sol, Ti♭, Re
C, E♭, G, B♭, D

Position A

III

Position B

IX

A	A♯	B	C	♯ or ♭	D	♯ or ♭	E	F	♯ or ♭	G	♯ or ♭	A
B	F	♯ or ♭	G	♯ or ♭	A	♯ or ♭	B	C	♯ or ♭	D	♯ or ♭	E
Fret	I	II	III	IV	V	VI	VII	VIII	IX	X	XI	XII

Dominant Seventh Minor Ninth Chord

The dominant seventh minor ninth chord is composed of the tonic, the third, the fifth, the minor seventh, and the minor ninth.

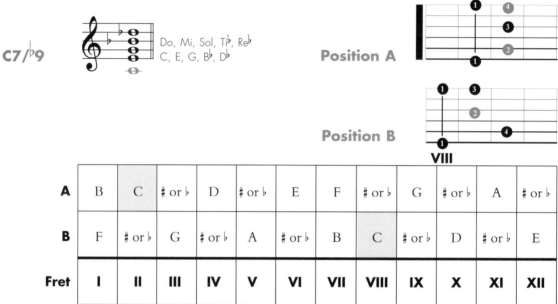

Dominant Seventh Augmented Ninth Chord

The dominant seventh augmented ninth chord is composed of the tonic, the third, the fifth, the dominant (minor) seventh, and the augmented ninth.

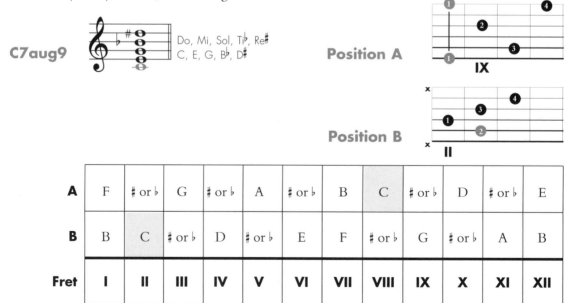

Ninth Diminished Fifth Chord

The ninth diminished fifth chord is composed of the tonic, the third, the diminished fifth, the minor seventh, and the ninth.

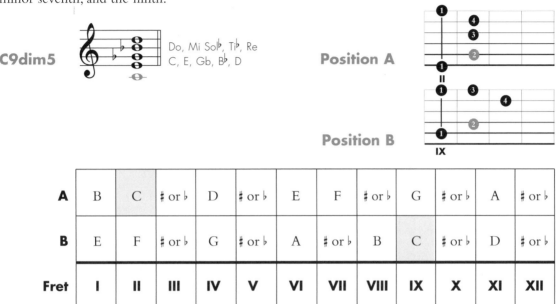

C9dim5

Do, Mi Solb, Tib, Re
C, E, Gb, Bb, D

Position A

Position B

	I	II	III	IV	V	VI	VII	VIII	IX	X	XI	XII
A	B	C	# or ♭	D	# or ♭	E	F	# or ♭	G	# or ♭	A	# or ♭
B	E	F	# or ♭	G	# or ♭	A	# or ♭	B	C	# or ♭	D	# or ♭
Fret	I	II	III	IV	V	VI	VII	VIII	IX	X	XI	XII

Ninth Augmented Fifth Chord

The ninth augmented fifth chord is composed of the tonic, the third, the augmented fifth, the minor seventh, and the ninth.

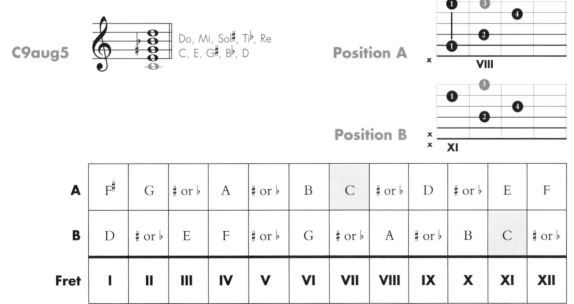

C9aug5

Do, Mi, Sol#, Tib, Re
C, E, G#, Bb, D

Position A

Position B

	I	II	III	IV	V	VI	VII	VIII	IX	X	XI	XII
A	F#	G	# or ♭	A	# or ♭	B	C	# or ♭	D	# or ♭	E	F
B	D	# or ♭	E	F	# or ♭	G	# or ♭	A	# or ♭	B	C	# or ♭
Fret	I	II	III	IV	V	VI	VII	VIII	IX	X	XI	XII

Major Ninth Chord

The major ninth chord is composed of the tonic, the third, the fifth, the major seventh, and the ninth.

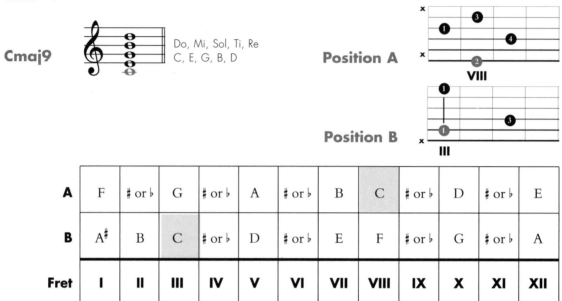

A	F	♯ or ♭	G	♯ or ♭	A	♯ or ♭	B	C	♯ or ♭	D	♯ or ♭	E
B	A♯	B	C	♯ or ♭	D	♯ or ♭	E	F	♯ or ♭	G	♯ or ♭	A
Fret	I	II	III	IV	V	VI	VII	VIII	IX	X	XI	XII

Minor Eleventh Chord

The minor eleventh chord is composed of the tonic, the minor third, the fifth, the minor seventh, the ninth, and the eleventh.

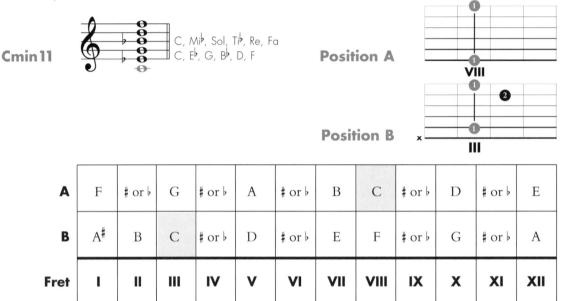

Cmin11

C, Mi♭, Sol, Ti♭, Re, Fa
C, E♭, G, B♭, D, F

Position A

Position B

A	F	# or ♭	G	# or ♭	A	# or ♭	B	C	# or ♭	D	# or ♭	E
B	A#	B	C	# or ♭	D	# or ♭	E	F	# or ♭	G	# or ♭	A
Fret	I	II	III	IV	V	VI	VII	VIII	IX	X	XI	XII

Eleventh Chord

The eleventh chord is composed of the tonic, the major third, the fifth, the minor seventh, the ninth, and the eleventh.

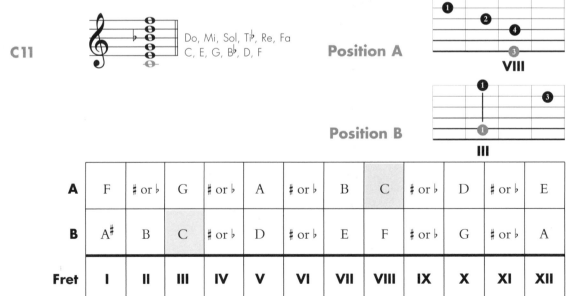

C11

Do, Mi, Sol, Ti♭, Re, Fa
C, E, G, B♭, D, F

Position A

Position B

A	F	# or ♭	G	# or ♭	A	# or ♭	B	C	# or ♭	D	# or ♭	E
B	A#	B	C	# or ♭	D	# or ♭	E	F	# or ♭	G	# or ♭	A
Fret	I	II	III	IV	V	VI	VII	VIII	IX	X	XI	XII

Seventh Augmented Eleventh Chord

The seventh augmented eleventh chord is composed of the tonic, the major third, the fifth, the minor seventh, the ninth, and the augmented eleventh.

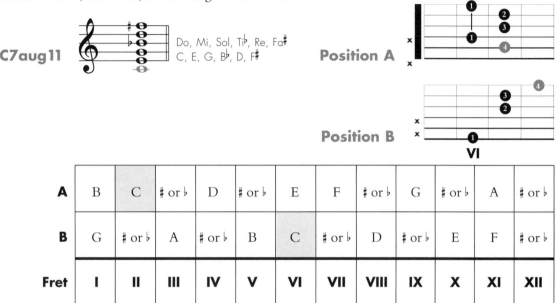

C7aug11

Do, Mi, Sol, Ti♭, Re, Fa♯
C, E, G, B♭, D, F♯

Position A

Position B

	I	II	III	IV	V	VI	VII	VIII	IX	X	XI	XII
A	B	C	♯ or ♭	D	♯ or ♭	E	F	♯ or ♭	G	♯ or ♭	A	♯ or ♭
B	G	♯ or ♭	A	♯ or ♭	B	C	♯ or ♭	D	♯ or ♭	E	F	♯ or ♭
Fret	I	II	III	IV	V	VI	VII	VIII	IX	X	XI	XII

Minor Thirteenth Chord

The minor thirteenth chord is composed of the tonic, the minor third, the fifth, the minor seventh, the ninth, the eleventh, and the thirteenth.

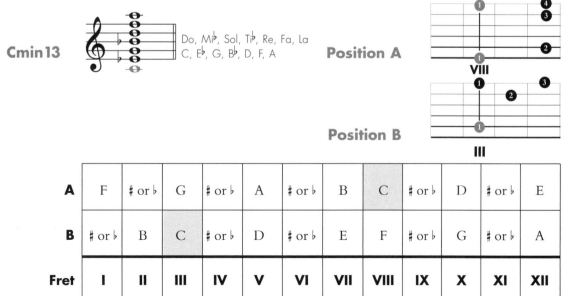

Cmin13

Do, Mi♭, Sol, Ti♭, Re, Fa, La
C, E♭, G, B♭, D, F, A

Position A

Position B

	I	II	III	IV	V	VI	VII	VIII	IX	X	XI	XII
A	F	♯ or ♭	G	♯ or ♭	A	♯ or ♭	B	C	♯ or ♭	D	♯ or ♭	E
B	♯ or ♭	B	C	♯ or ♭	D	♯ or ♭	E	F	♯ or ♭	G	♯ or ♭	A
Fret	I	II	III	IV	V	VI	VII	VIII	IX	X	XI	XII

Thirteenth Chord

The thirteenth chord is composed of the tonic, the third, the fifth, the minor seventh, the ninth, the eleventh, and the thirteenth.

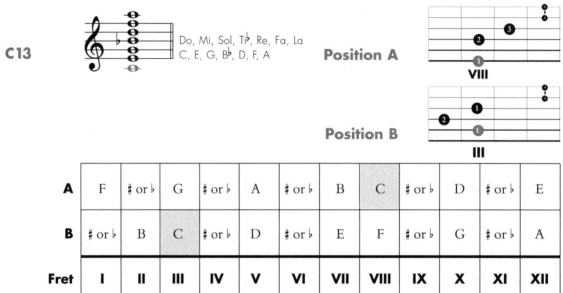

A	F	♯ or ♭	G	♯ or ♭	A	♯ or ♭	B	C	♯ or ♭	D	♯ or ♭	E
B	♯ or ♭	B	C	♯ or ♭	D	♯ or ♭	E	F	♯ or ♭	G	♯ or ♭	A
Fret	I	II	III	IV	V	VI	VII	VIII	IX	X	XI	XII

Chapter 5

Chord Dictionary

In this Chord Dictionary you'll find the appropriate fingering shown on the guitar fingerboard for chords built on all twelve tones. Please see the Guide to Music Notation below.

Guide to Music Notation

Here is a guide to standard music notation. We use C as an example. Any of the other eleven tones of the chromatic scale can be substituted for C in this table.

Caug	C augmented (also notated as C+) refers to a chord with a major third and an augmented fifth.
C6	C major chord with an added major sixth.
Cmin6	C minor chord with an added major sixth (also notated Cm6).
C6add9	C major chord with an added major sixth and an added major ninth (also notated C6/9).
C7	C major chord with a minor seventh (also called C dominant seventh).
Cmin7	C minor chord with a minor seventh (also notated Cm7).
Cmin7/♭5	C chord with a minor third, minor seventh, and diminished fifth (also notated Cm7-5).
Cmaj7	C major chord with a major seventh.
Cdim7	C diminished chord with a diminished seventh (also notated as C°7 in some cases).
C7/♯5	C chord with a minor seventh and an augmented fifth.
Cmin/maj7	C minor chord with a major seventh (also notated Cm/maj7).
C7sus	C major chord with a minor seventh; the third is replaced by the fourth "suspended" and resolved downward to the third on a later beat; *sus* always means a suspended fourth (also notated Cm7sus or Cm7sus4).
Cmin7sus	C minor chord with minor seventh; the third is replaced by the fourth "suspended" and resolved downward to the third on a later beat; *sus* always means a suspended fourth (also notated as Cm7sus or Cm7sus4).
C9	C major with minor seventh and added major ninth.
Cmaj7add9	C major chord with major seventh and added major ninth (also notated Cmaj7/9 or Cmaj9).
Cmin9	C minor chord with minor seventh and added ninth (also notated Cm9).
C11	C major chord with minor seventh and added major ninth and major eleventh.
C13	C major chord with minor seventh and added major ninth and major thirteenth.

Chords Built on
C (Do)

C Major

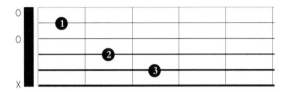

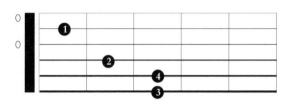

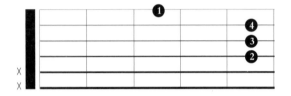

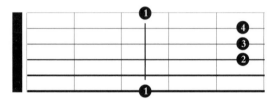

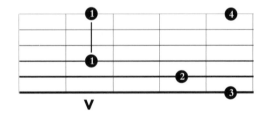

V

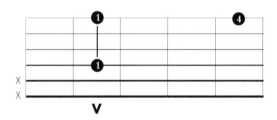

V

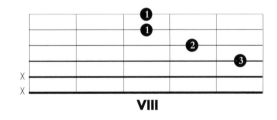

VIII

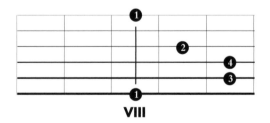

VIII

C Minor

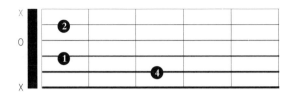

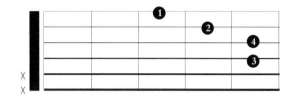

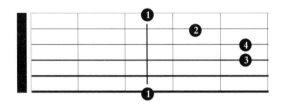

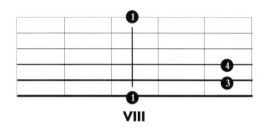

VIII

Caug

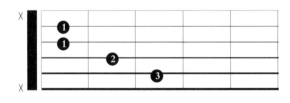

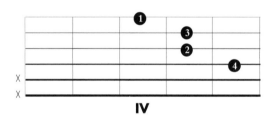

IV

C6

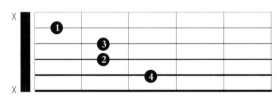

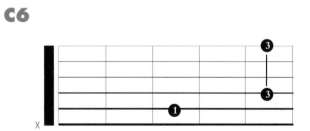

C6

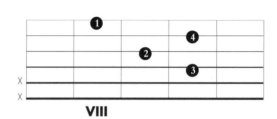

VII

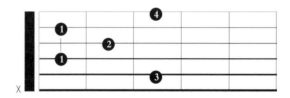

VIII

Cmin6

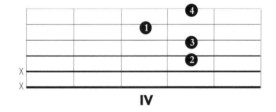

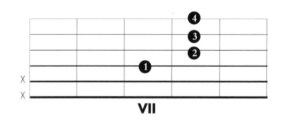

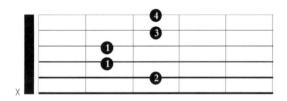

IV

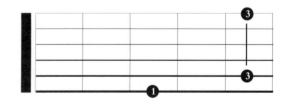

VII

C6add9

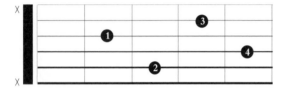

C6add9

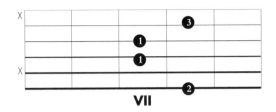

VII

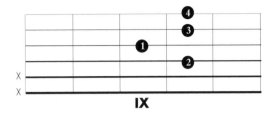

IX

C7

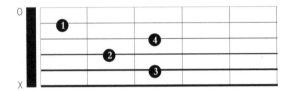

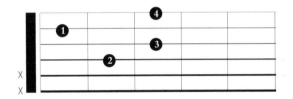

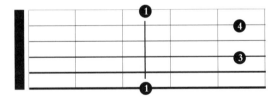

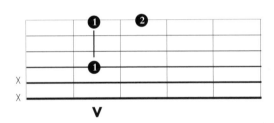

V

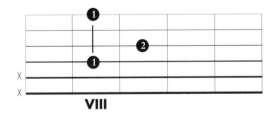

VIII

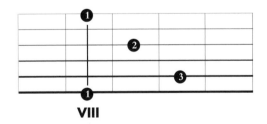

VIII

C7

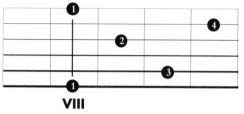

VIII

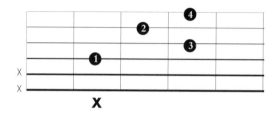

X

Cmin7

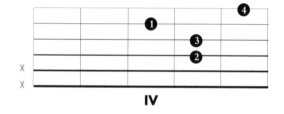

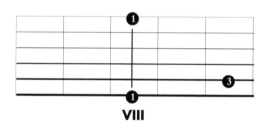

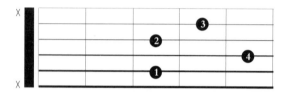

IV

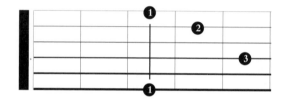

VIII

Cmin7/♭5

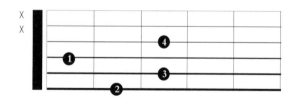

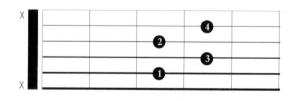

Cmin7/♭5

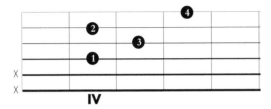

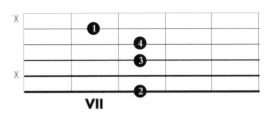

IV   VII

Cmaj7

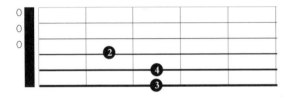

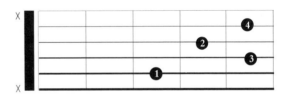

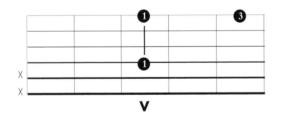

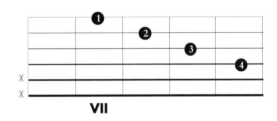

V   VII

Cdim7

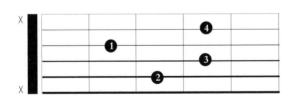

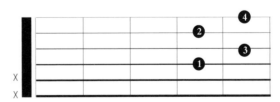

Cdim7

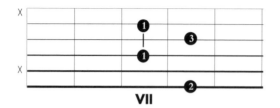

VII

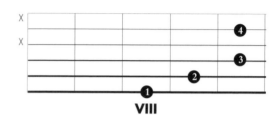

VIII

C7/#5

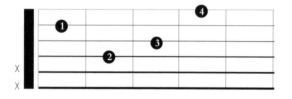

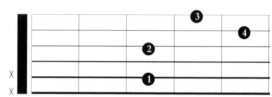

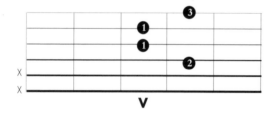

V

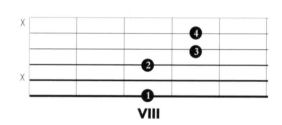

VIII

Cmin/maj7

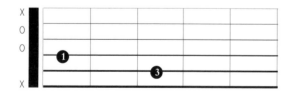

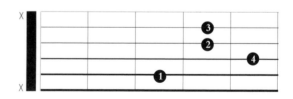

Cmin/maj7

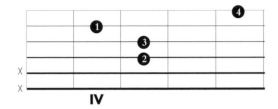

IV

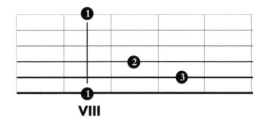

VIII

C7sus

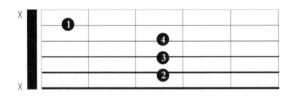

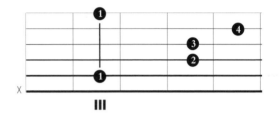

III

Cmin7sus

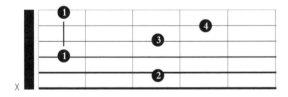

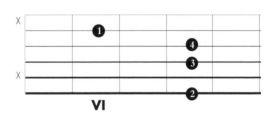

VI

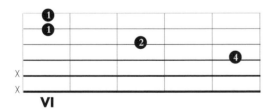

VI

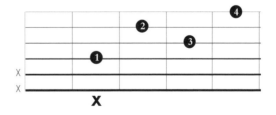

X

C9

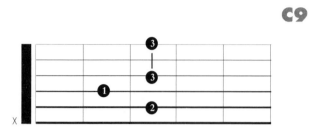

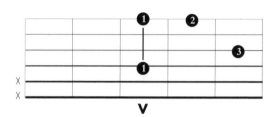

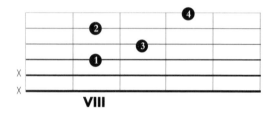

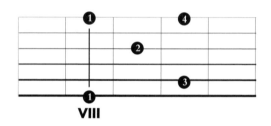

Cmaj7add9

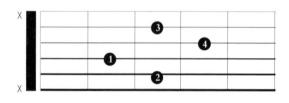

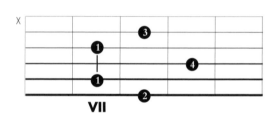

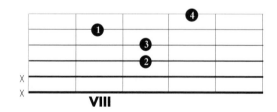

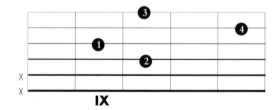

Cmin9

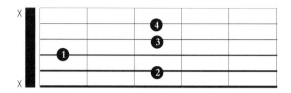

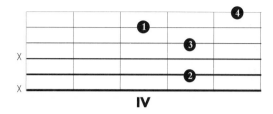
IV

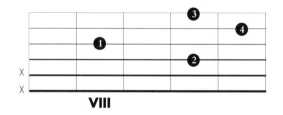
VIII

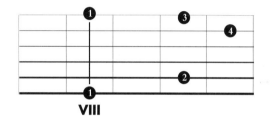
VIII

C11

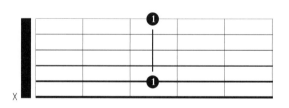
X

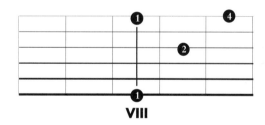
VIII

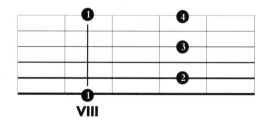
VIII

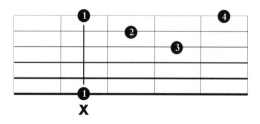
X

C13

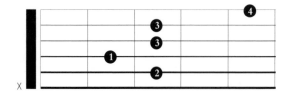

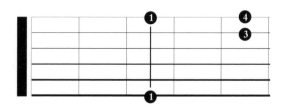

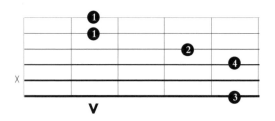

V

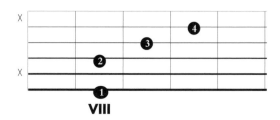

VIII

Chords Built on
C# or Db
(Do# or Reb)

C# Major or D♭ Major

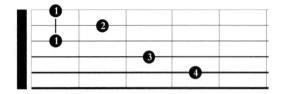

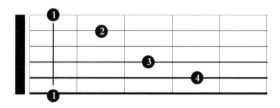

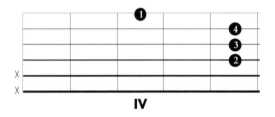

IV

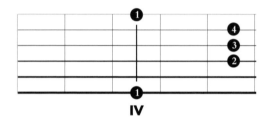

IV

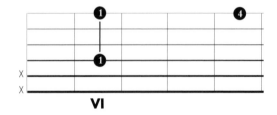

VI

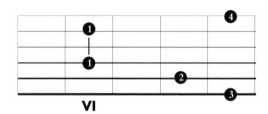

VI

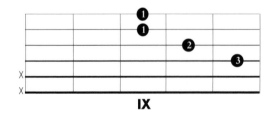

IX

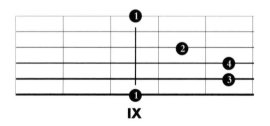

IX

C# Minor or D♭ Minor

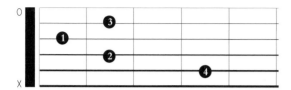

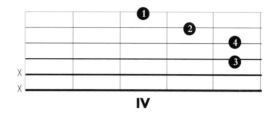

IV

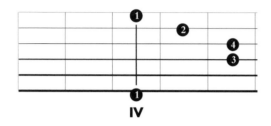

IV

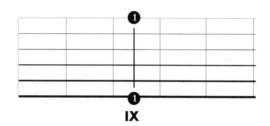

IX

C#aug or D♭aug

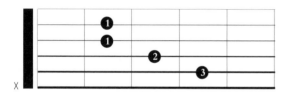

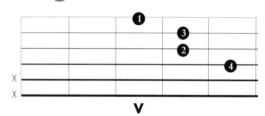

V

C#6 or D♭6

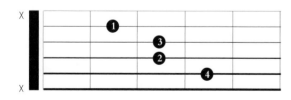

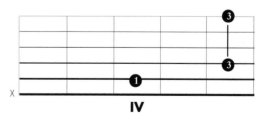

IV

C#6 or Db6

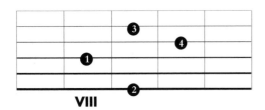

VIII

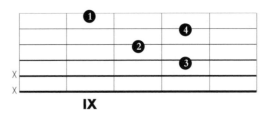

IX

C#min6 or Dbmin6

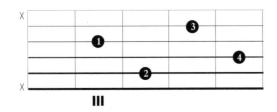

III

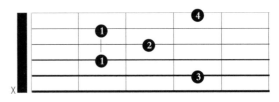

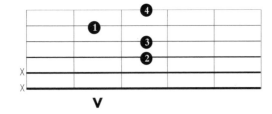

V

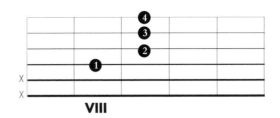

VIII

C#6add9 or Db6add9

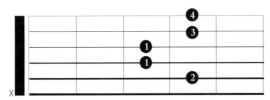

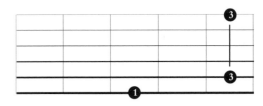

C#6add9 or Db6add9

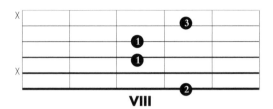

VIII

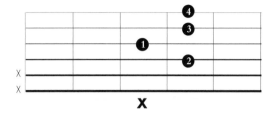

X

C#7 or Db7

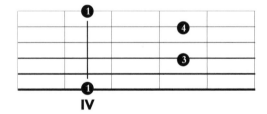

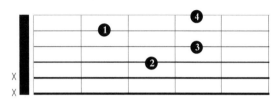

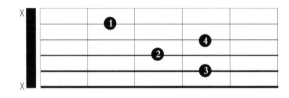

IV

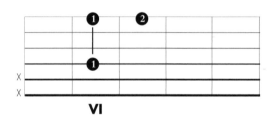

VI

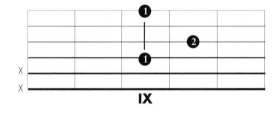

IX

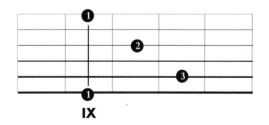

IX

C#7 or Db7

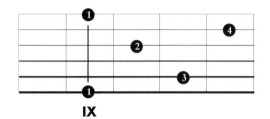

IX

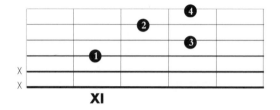

XI

C#min7 or Dbmin7

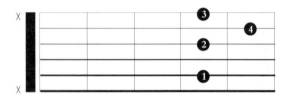

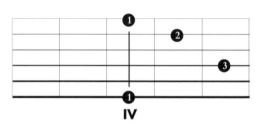

IV

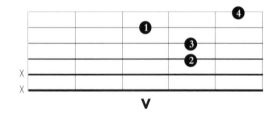

V

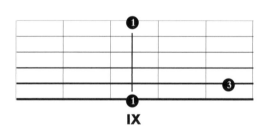

IX

C#min7/b5 or Dbmin7/b5

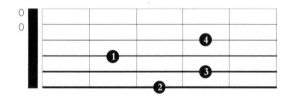

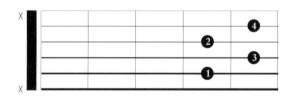

C#min7/b5 or Dbmin7/b5

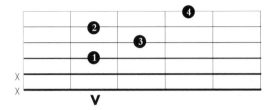

V

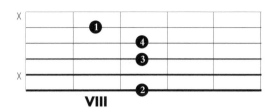

VIII

C#maj7 or Dbmaj7

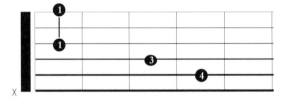

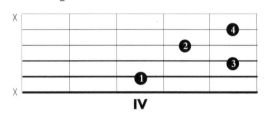

IV

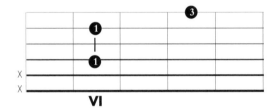

VI

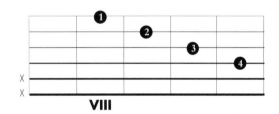

VIII

C#dim7

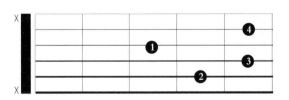

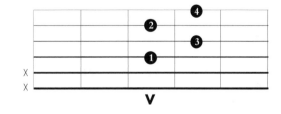

V

C#dim7 or D♭dim7

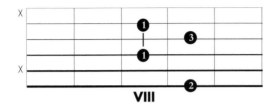

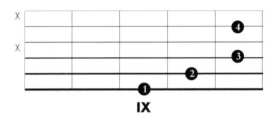

C#7/#5 or D♭7/#5

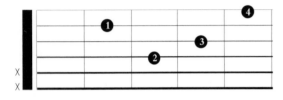

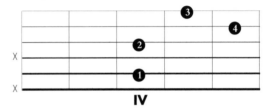

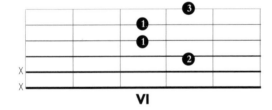

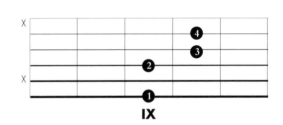

C#min/maj7 or D♭min/maj7

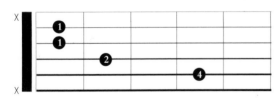

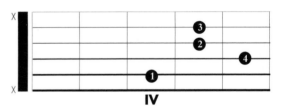

C#min/maj7 or Dbmin/maj7

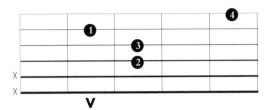

V

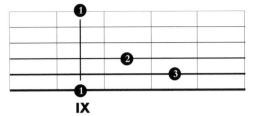

IX

C#7sus or Db7sus

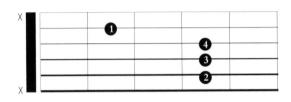

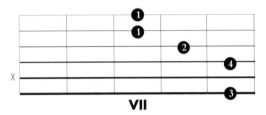

VII

C#min7sus or Dbmin7sus

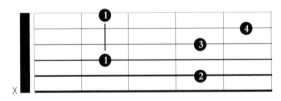

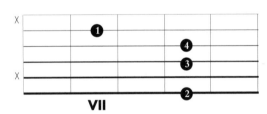

VII

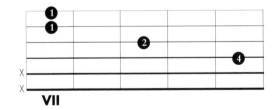

VII

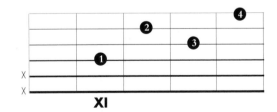

XI

C#9 or Db9

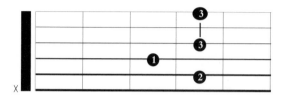

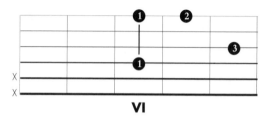

VI

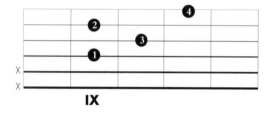

IX

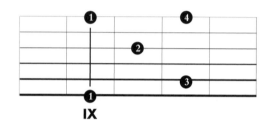

IX

C#maj7add9 or Dbmaj7add9

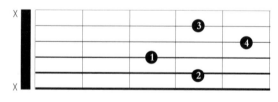

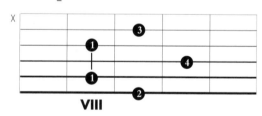

VIII

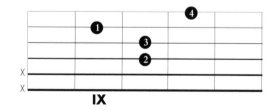

IX

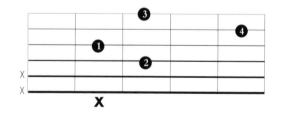

X

C#min9 or D♭min9

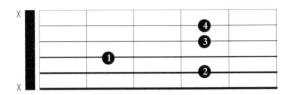

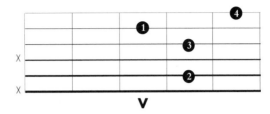

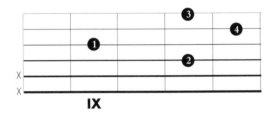

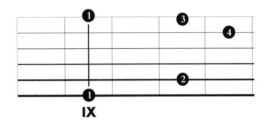

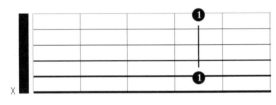

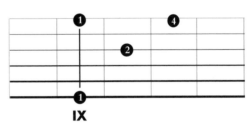

C#11 or D♭11

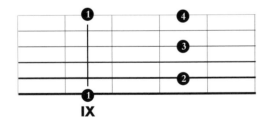

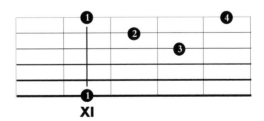

C#13 or Db13

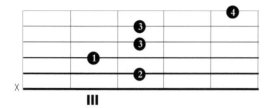

III

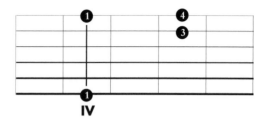

IV

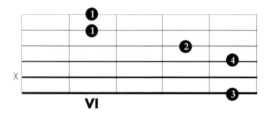

VI

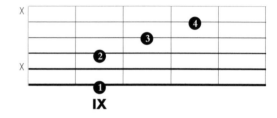

IX

Chords Built on D (Re)

D Major

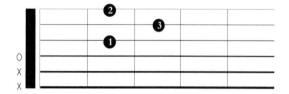

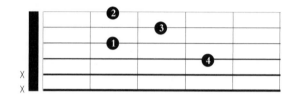

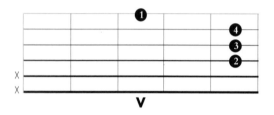

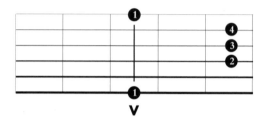

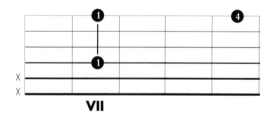

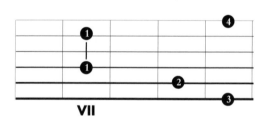

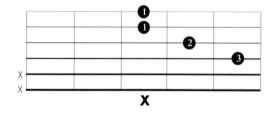

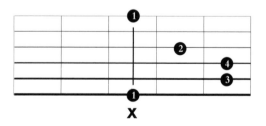

D Minor

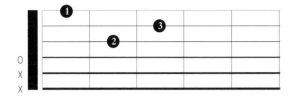

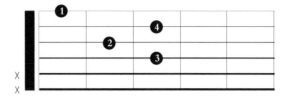

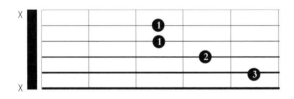

V

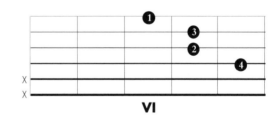

X

Daug

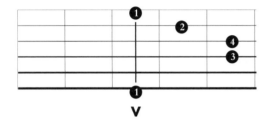

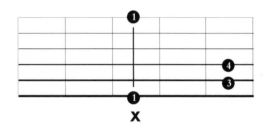

VI

D6

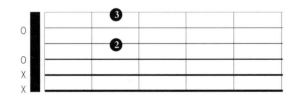

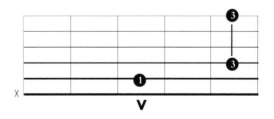

V

D6

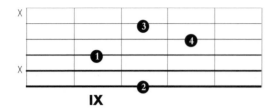

IX

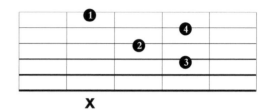

X

Dmin6

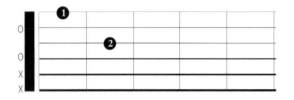

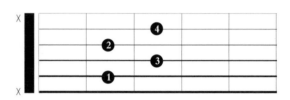

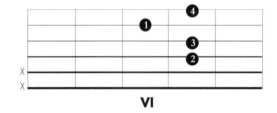

VI

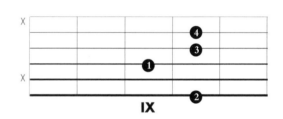

IX

D6add9

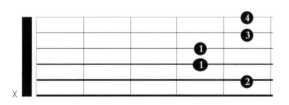

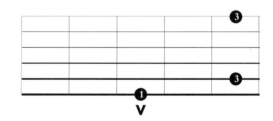

V

D6add9

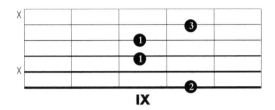

IX

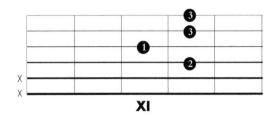

XI

D7

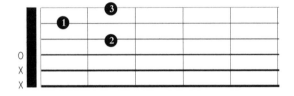

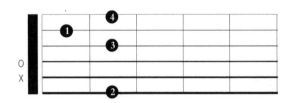

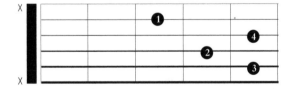

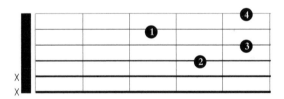

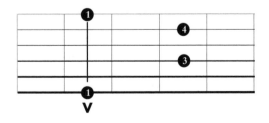

V

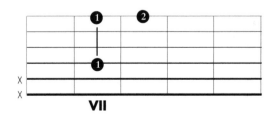

VII

D7

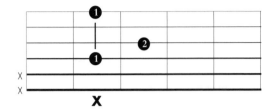

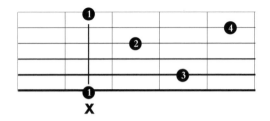

Dmin7

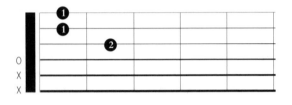

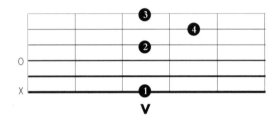

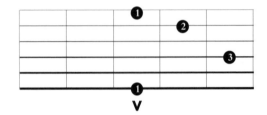

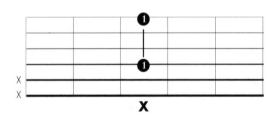

Dmin7/♭5

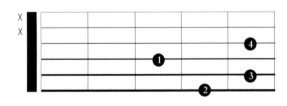

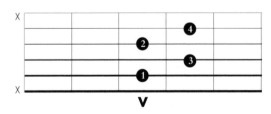

Dmin7/♭5

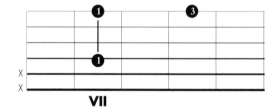

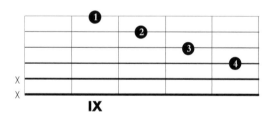

Dmaj7

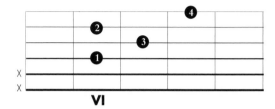

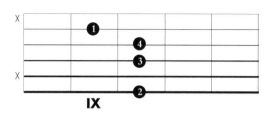

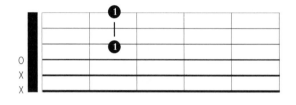

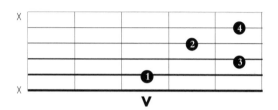

Ddim7

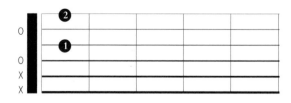

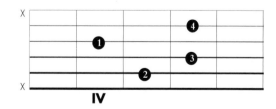

Ddim7

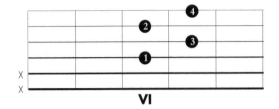

VI

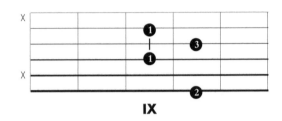

IX

D7/#5

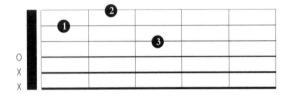

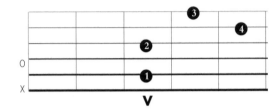

V

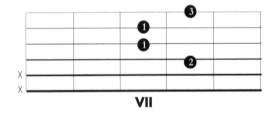

VII

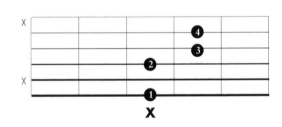

X

Dmin/maj7

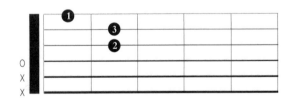

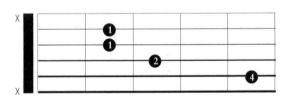

Dmin/maj7

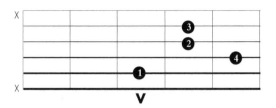
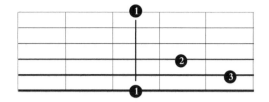

D7sus

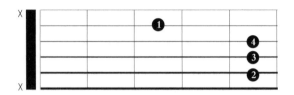
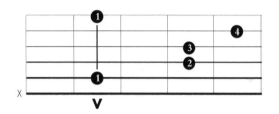

Dmin7sus

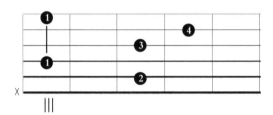
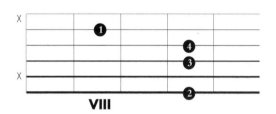

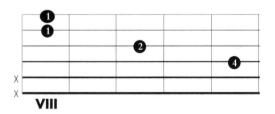
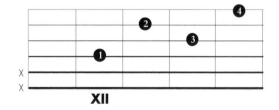

D9

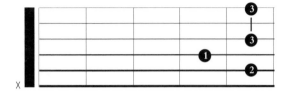

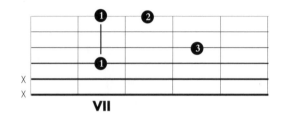

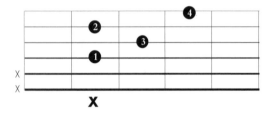

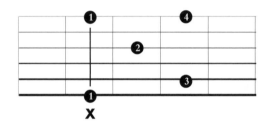

Dmaj7add9

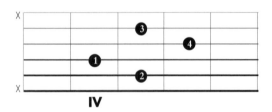

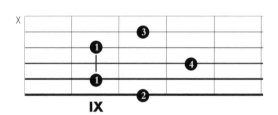

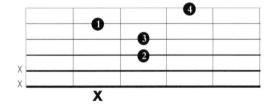

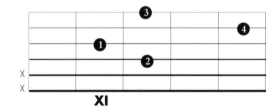

Dmin9

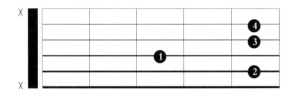

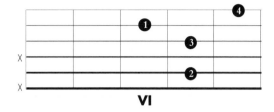

VI

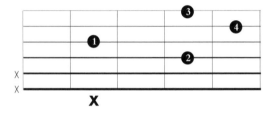

X

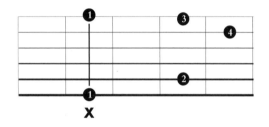

X

D11

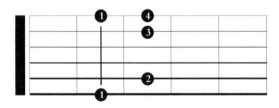

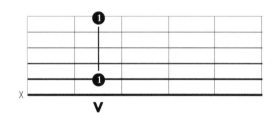

V

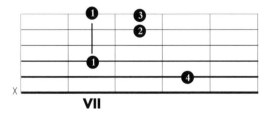

VII

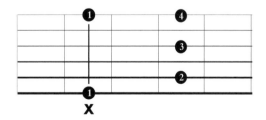

X

D13

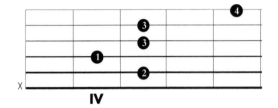

IV

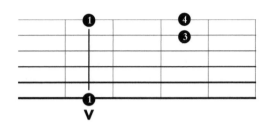

V

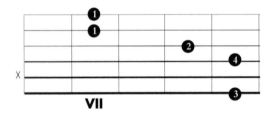

VII

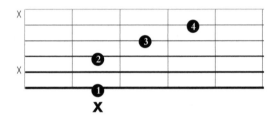

X

Chords Built on E♭ (Mi♭)

E♭ Major

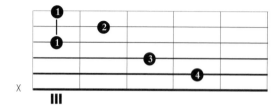

III

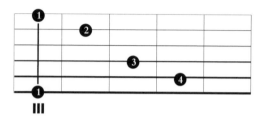

III

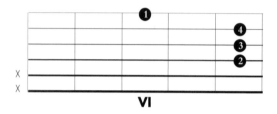

VI

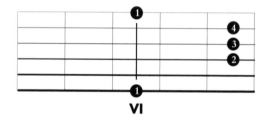

VI

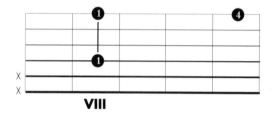

VIII

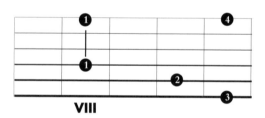

VIII

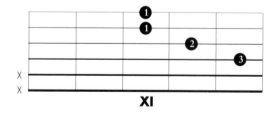

XI

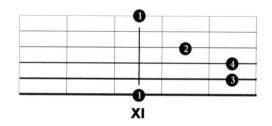

XI

E♭ Minor

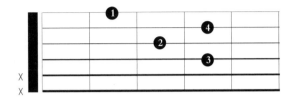

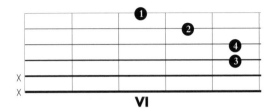

VI

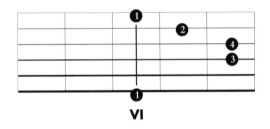

VI

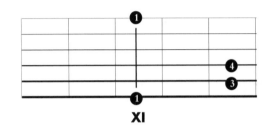

XI

E♭aug

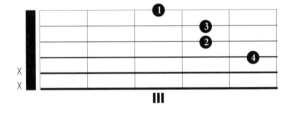

III

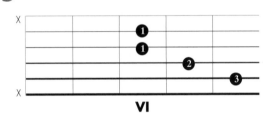

VI

E♭6

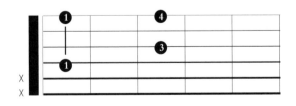

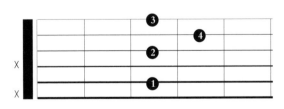

E♭6

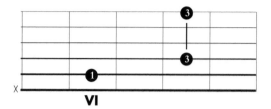

VI

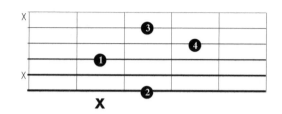

X

E♭min6

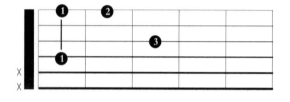

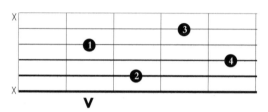

V

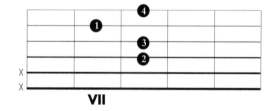

VII

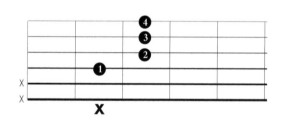

X

E♭6add9

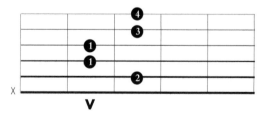

V

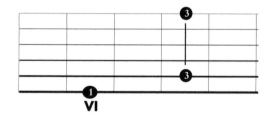

VI

E♭6add9

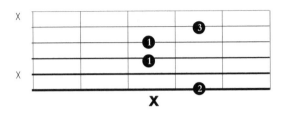

X

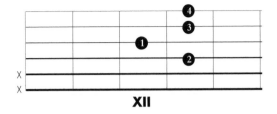

XII

E♭7

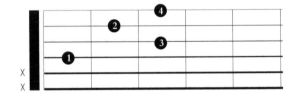

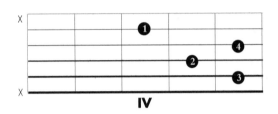

IV

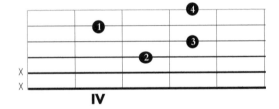

IV

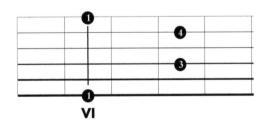

VI

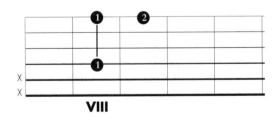

VIII

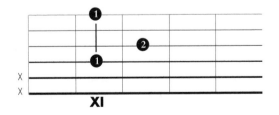

XI

E♭7

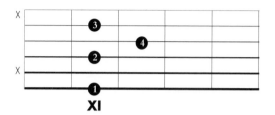

XI

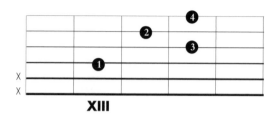

XIII

E♭min7

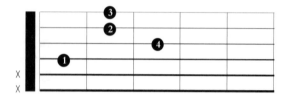

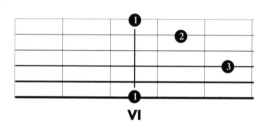

VI

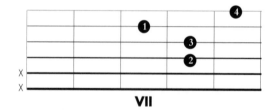

VII

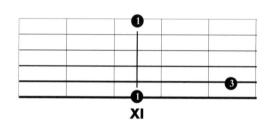

XI

E♭min7/♭5

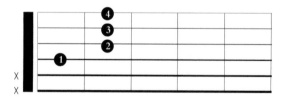

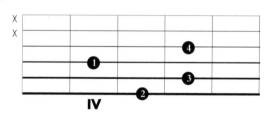

IV

E♭min7/♭5

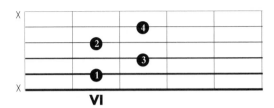

VI

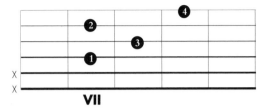

VII

E♭maj7

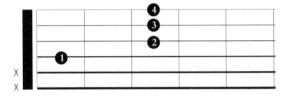

VI

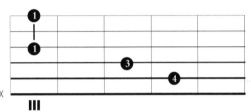

III

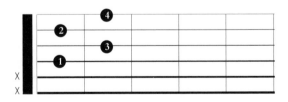

VI

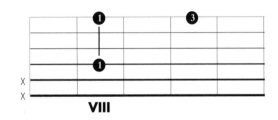

VIII

E♭dim7

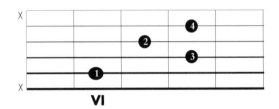

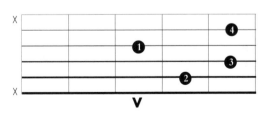

V

E♭dim7

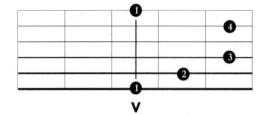

V

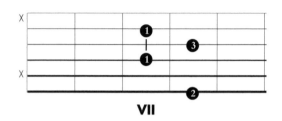

VII

E♭7/#5

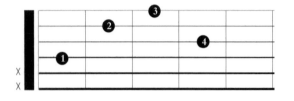

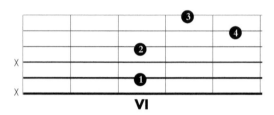

VI

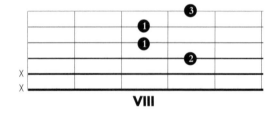

VIII

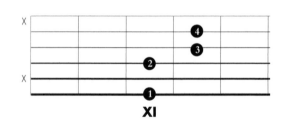

XI

E♭min/maj7

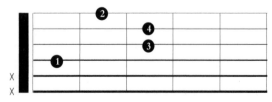

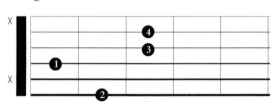

E♭min/maj7

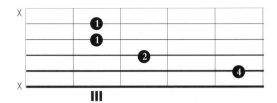

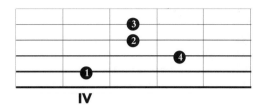

E♭7sus

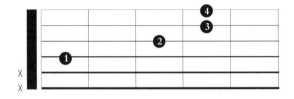

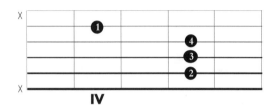

E♭min7sus

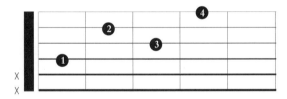

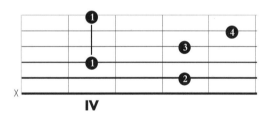

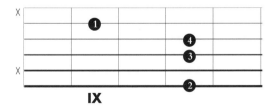

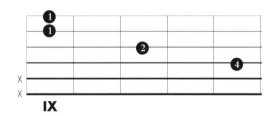

E♭9

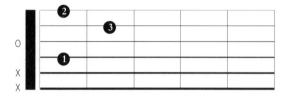

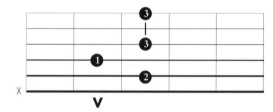

V

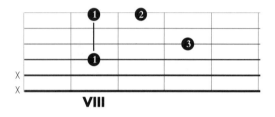

VIII

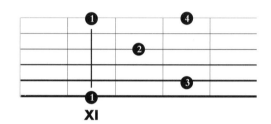

XI

E♭maj7add9

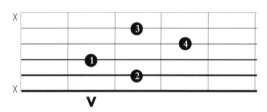

V

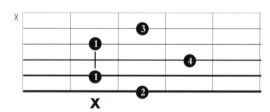

X

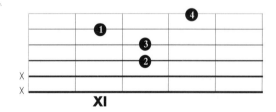

XI

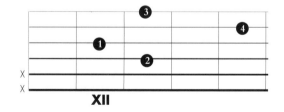

XII

E♭min9

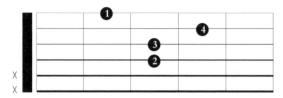

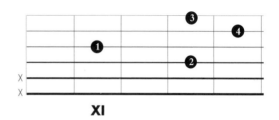

IV

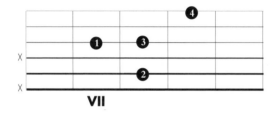

VII

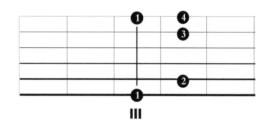

XI

E♭11

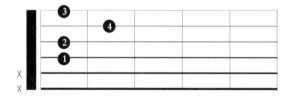

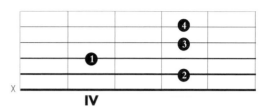

III

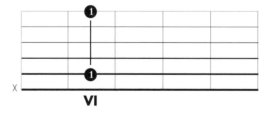

VI

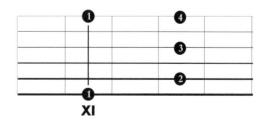

XI

E♭13

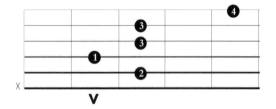

V

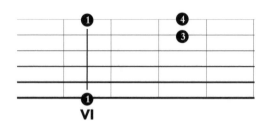

VI

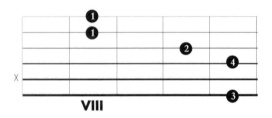

VIII

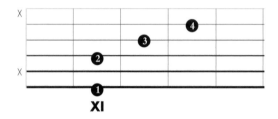

XI

Chords Built on
E (Mi)

E Major

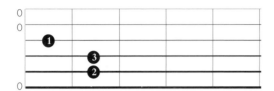

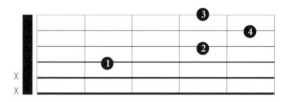

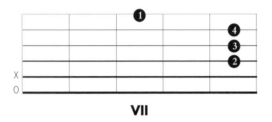

VII

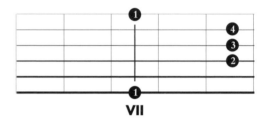

VII

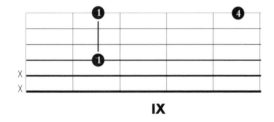

IX

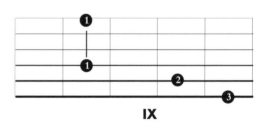

IX

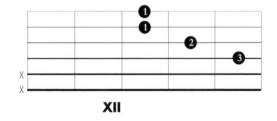

XII

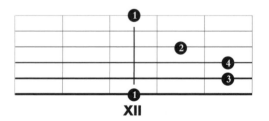

XII

E Minor

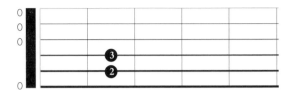 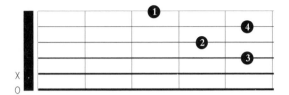

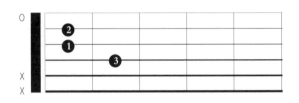
VII

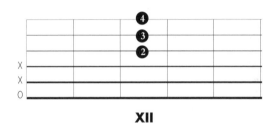
XII

Eaug

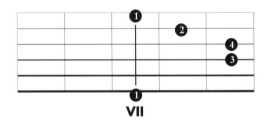

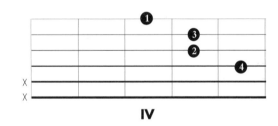
IV

E6

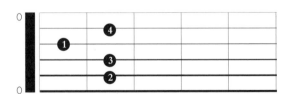 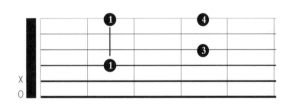

E6

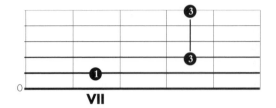

VII

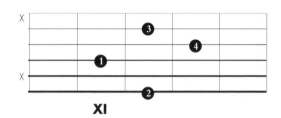

XI

Emin6

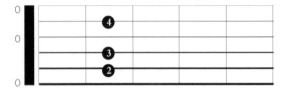

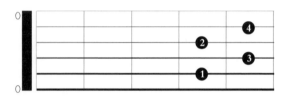

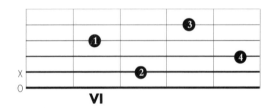

VI

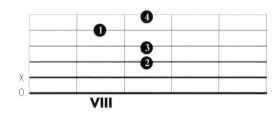

VIII

E6add9

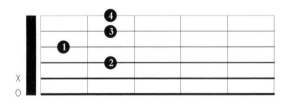

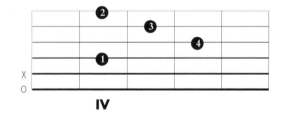

IV

E6add9

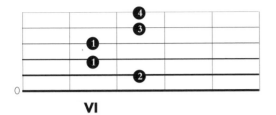

VI

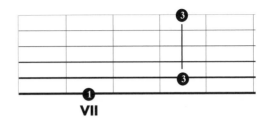

VII

E7

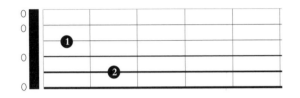

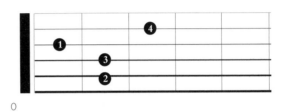

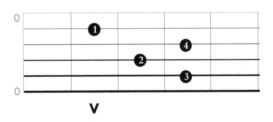

V

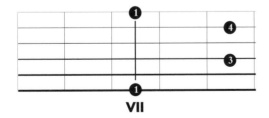

VII

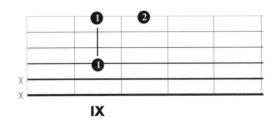

IX

E7

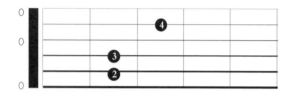

XII

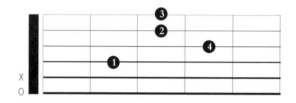

XII

Emin7

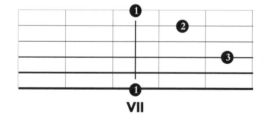

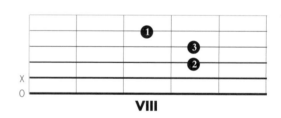

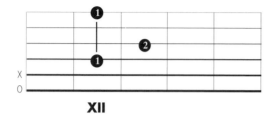

VII

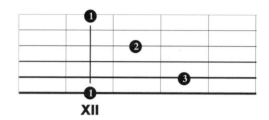

VIII

Emin7/♭5

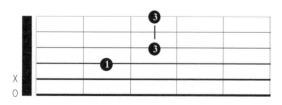

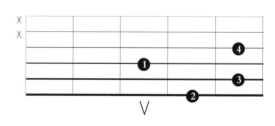

V

Emin7/♭5

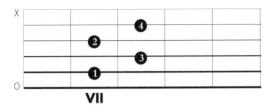

VII

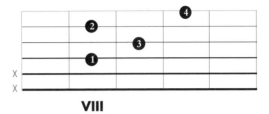

VIII

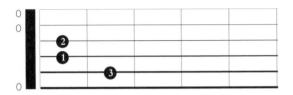

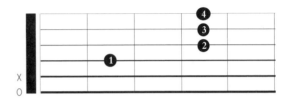

Emaj7

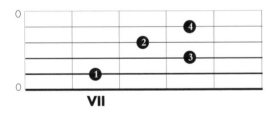

VII

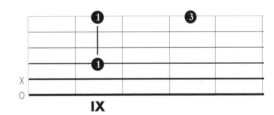

IX

Edim7

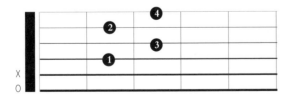

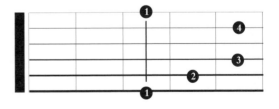

Edim7

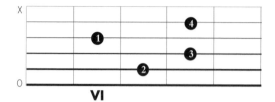

VI

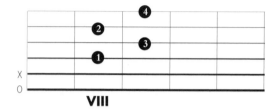

VIII

E7/#5

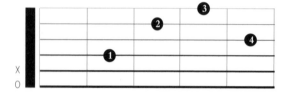

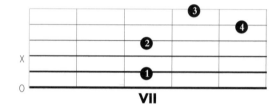

VII

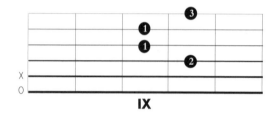

IX

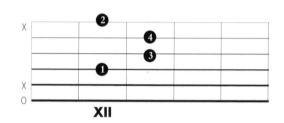

XII

Emin/maj7

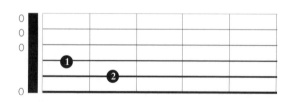

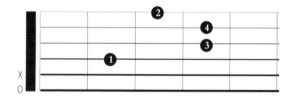

Emin/maj7

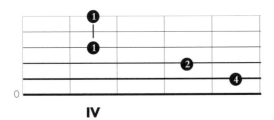

IV

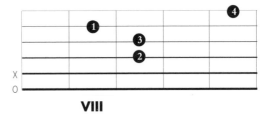

VIII

E7sus

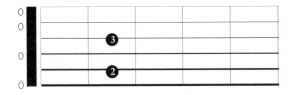

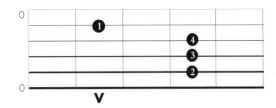

V

Emin7sus

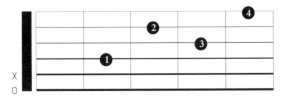

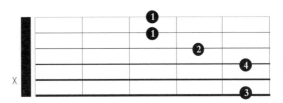

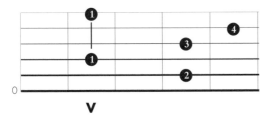

V

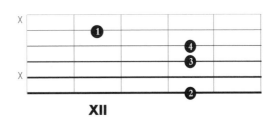

XII

E9

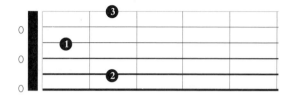

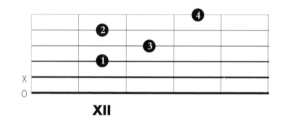

VI

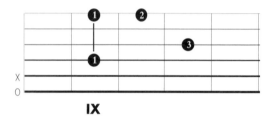

IX

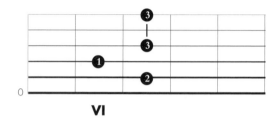

XII

Emaj7add9

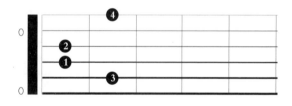

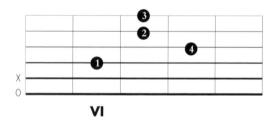

VI

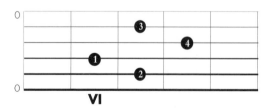

VI

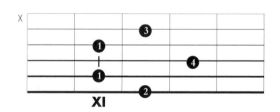

XI

Emin9

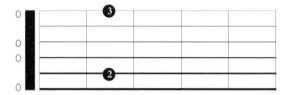

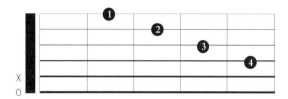

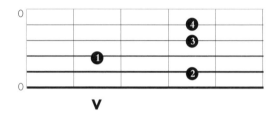

V

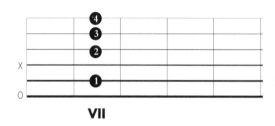

VII

E11

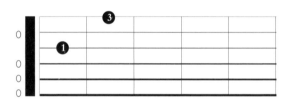

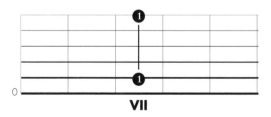

VII

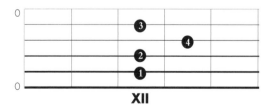

XII

E13

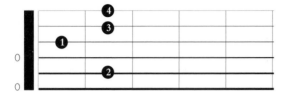

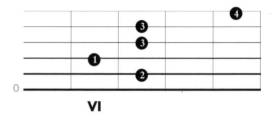

VI

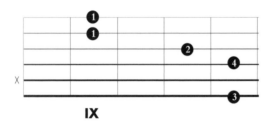

IX

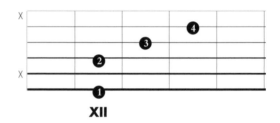

XII

Chords Built on
F (Fa)

F Major

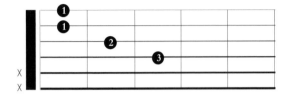

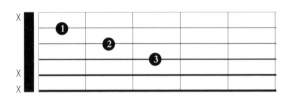

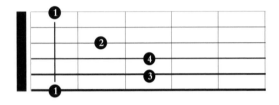

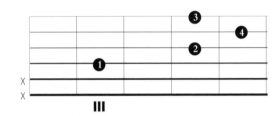

III

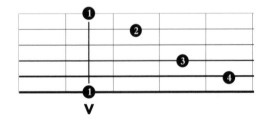

V

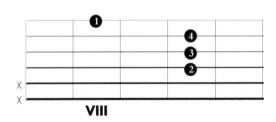

VIII

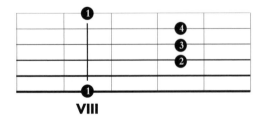

VIII

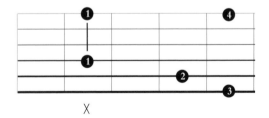

X

F Minor

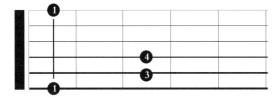

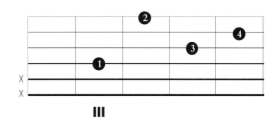

III

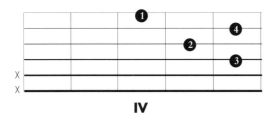

IV

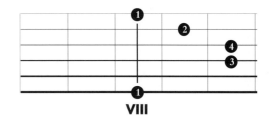

VIII

Faug

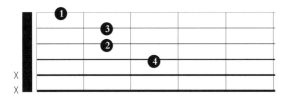

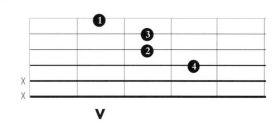

V

F6

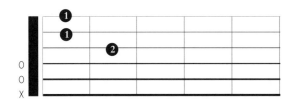

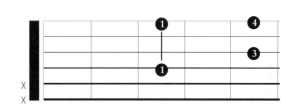

F6

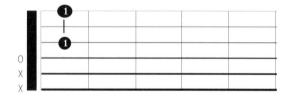

V

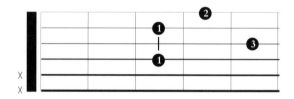

VIII

Fmin6

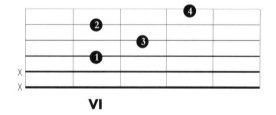

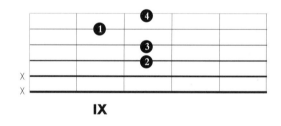

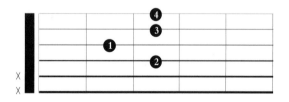

VI

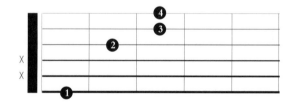

IX

F6add9

F6add9

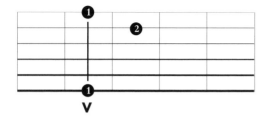

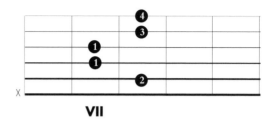

F7

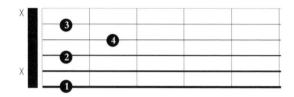

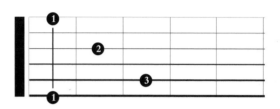

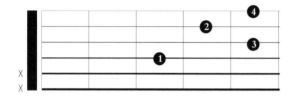

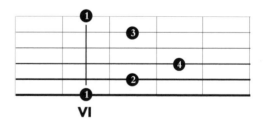

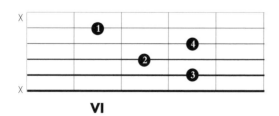

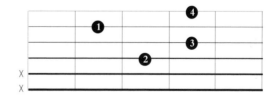

F7

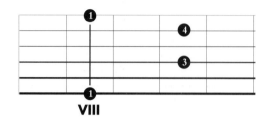

VIII

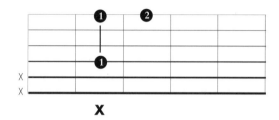

X

Fmin7

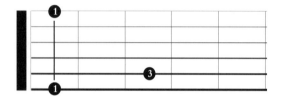

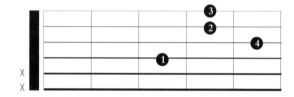

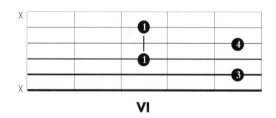

VI

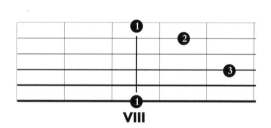

VIII

Fmin7/♭5

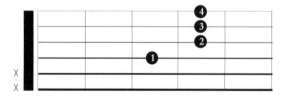

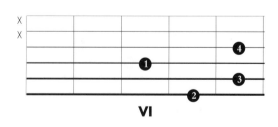

VI

Fmin7/♭5

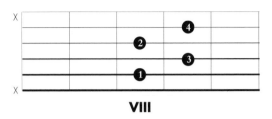

VIII

IX

Fmaj7

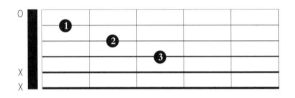

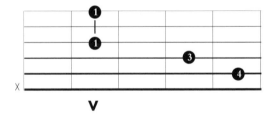

V

X

Fdim7

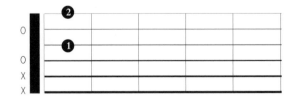

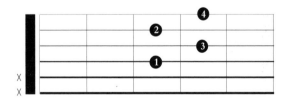

Fdim7

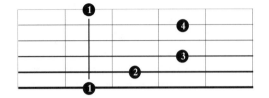

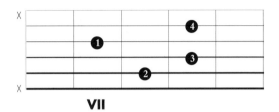

VII

F7/#5

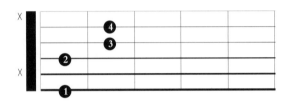

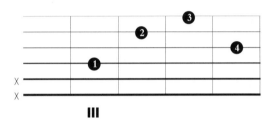

III

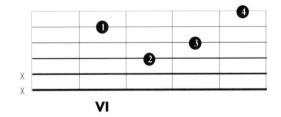

VI

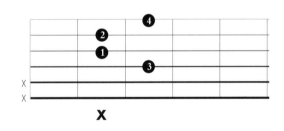

X

Fmin/maj7

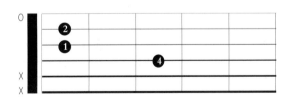

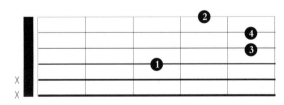

Fmin/maj7

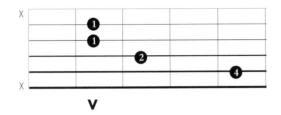

V

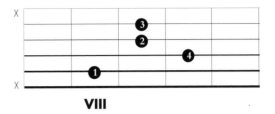

VIII

F7sus

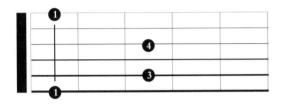

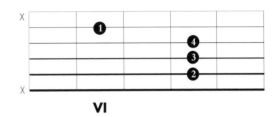

VI

Fmin7sus

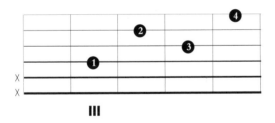

III

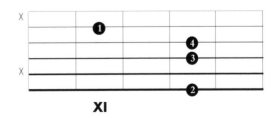

IV

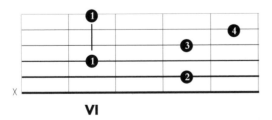

VI

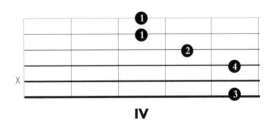

XI

F9

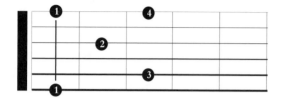

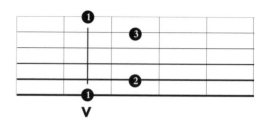

V

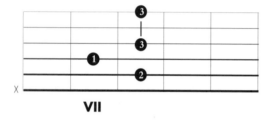

VII

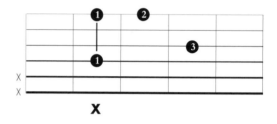

X

Fmaj7add9

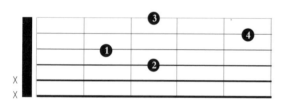

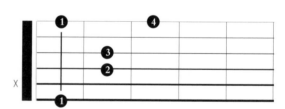

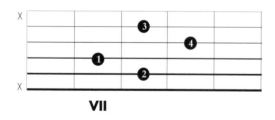

VII

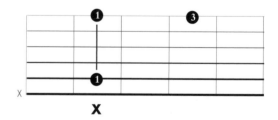

X

Fmin9

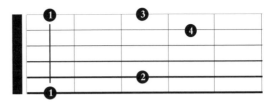

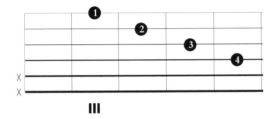

III

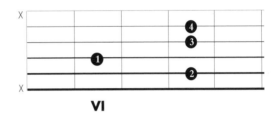

VI

F11

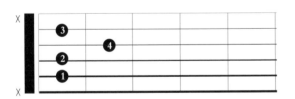

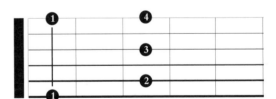

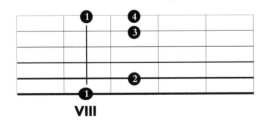

VIII

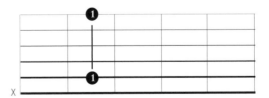

F13

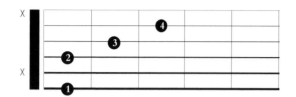

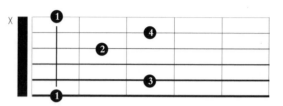

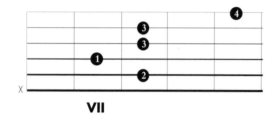

VII

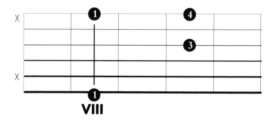

VIII

Chords Built on F# or Gb
(Fa# or Solb)

F# Major or Gb Major

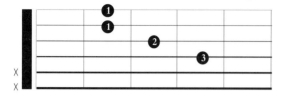

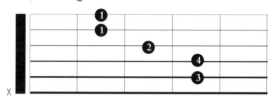

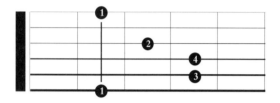

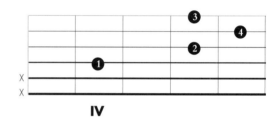

IV

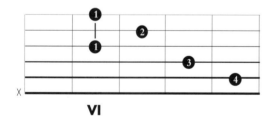

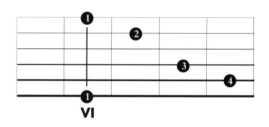

VI

VI

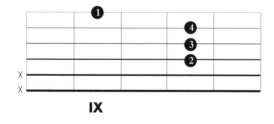

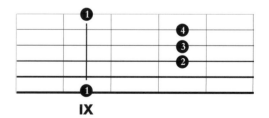

IX

IX

F#Minor or Gb Minor

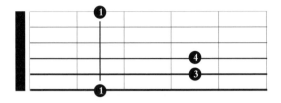

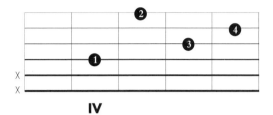

IV

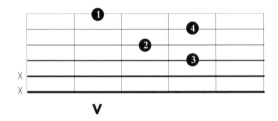

V

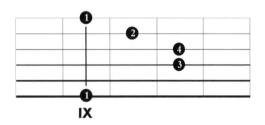

IX

F#aug or Gbaug

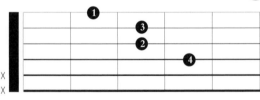

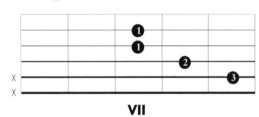

VII

F#6 or Gb6

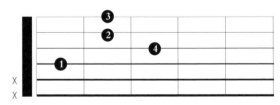

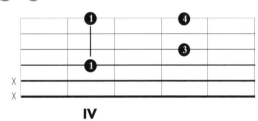

IV

F#6 or Gb6

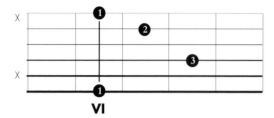

VI

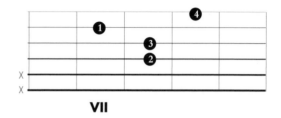

VII

F#minb or Gbmin6

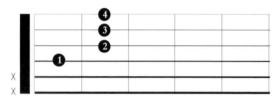

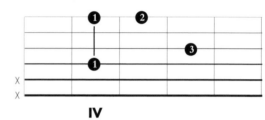

IV

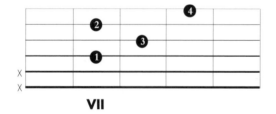

VII

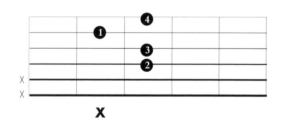

X

F#6add9 or Gb6add9

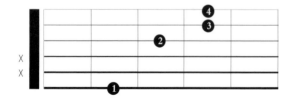

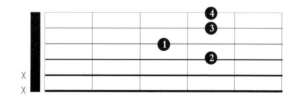

F#6add9 or Gb6add9

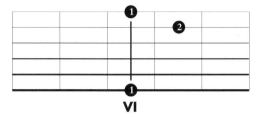

VI

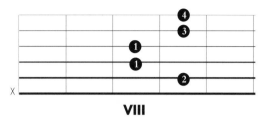

VIII

F#7 or Gb7

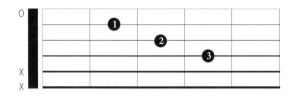

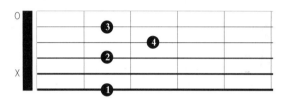

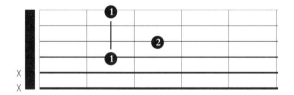

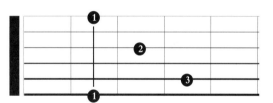

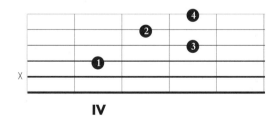

IV

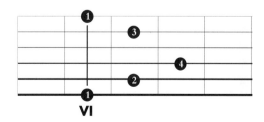

VI

F#7 or Gb7

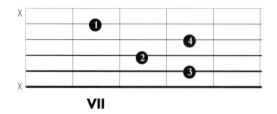

VII

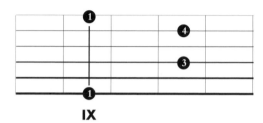

IX

F#min7 or Gbmin7

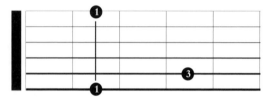

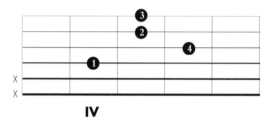

IV

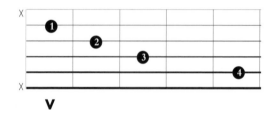

V

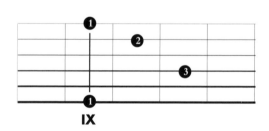

IX

F#min7/b5 or Gbmin7/b5

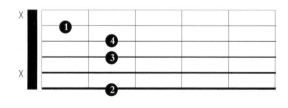

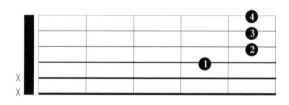

F#min7/b5 or Gbmin7/b5

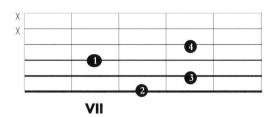

VII

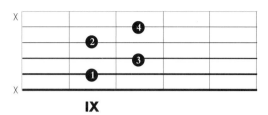

IX

F#maj7 or Gbmaj7

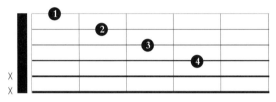

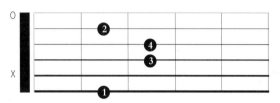

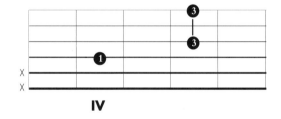

IV

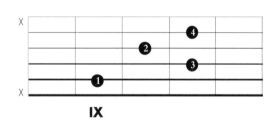

IX

F#dim7 or Gbdim7

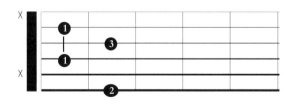

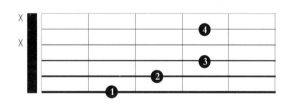

F#dim7 or Gbdim7

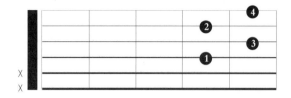

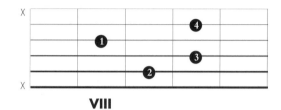

VIII

F#7/#5 or Gb7/#5

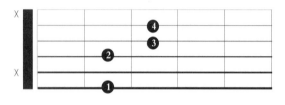

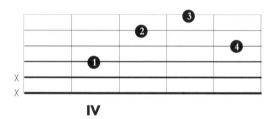

IV

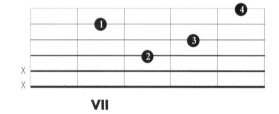

VII

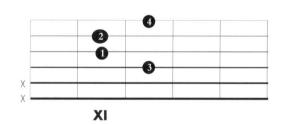

XI

F#min/maj7 or Gbmin/maj7

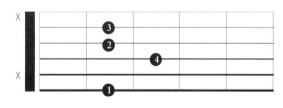

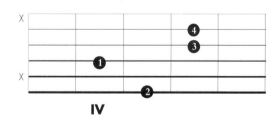

IV

F#min/maj7 or G♭min/maj7

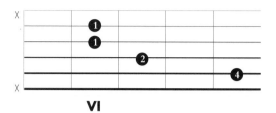

VI

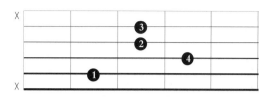

F#7sus or G♭7sus

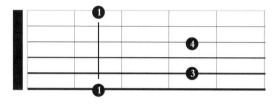

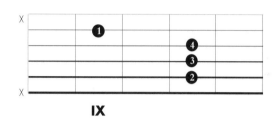

IX

F#min7sus or G♭min7sus

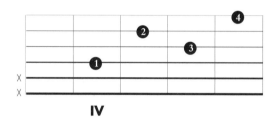

IV

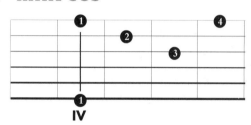

IV

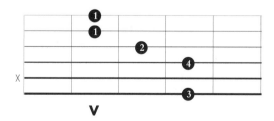

V

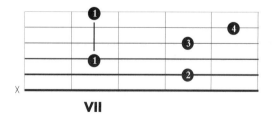

VII

F#9 or Gb9

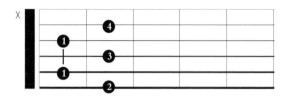

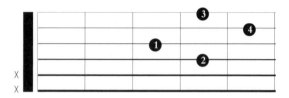

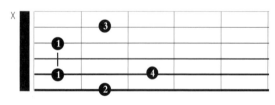
VI

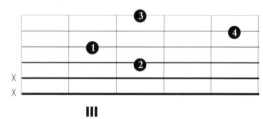
VIII

F#maj7add9 or Gbmaj7add9

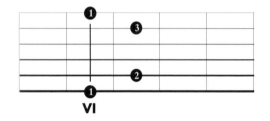

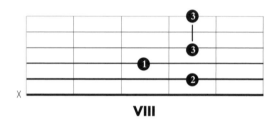
III

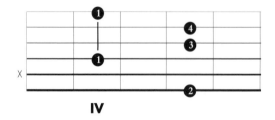
IV

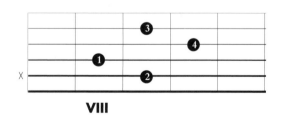
VIII

F#min9 or Gbmin9

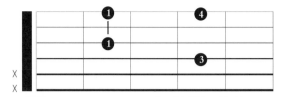

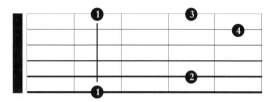

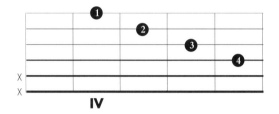

IV

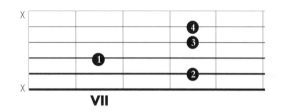

VII

F#11 or Gb11

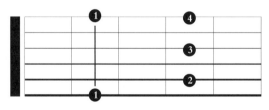

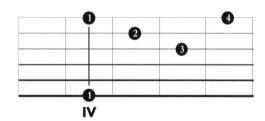

IV

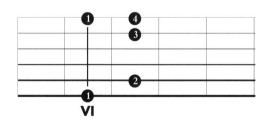

VI

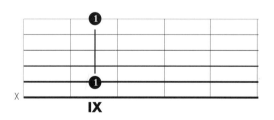

IX

F#13 or Gb13

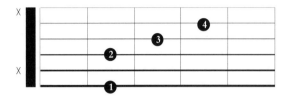

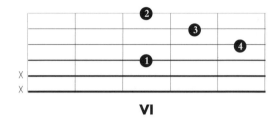

VI

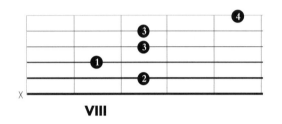

VIII

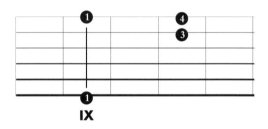

IX

Chords Built on G (Sol)

G Major

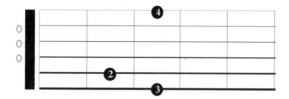

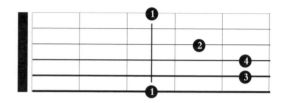

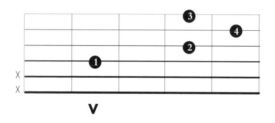

V

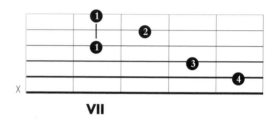

VII

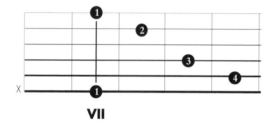

VII

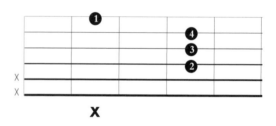

X

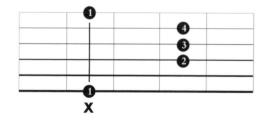

X

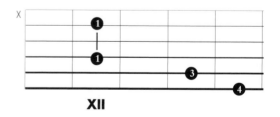

XII

G Minor

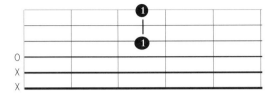
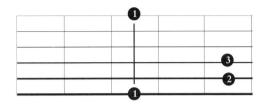

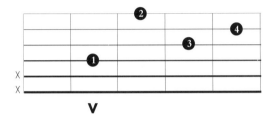
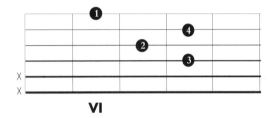

V

VI

Gaug

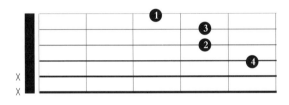
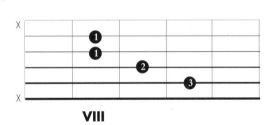

VIII

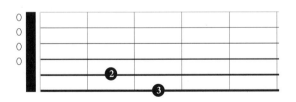
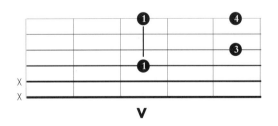

V

G6

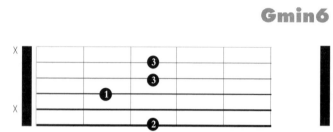

VII

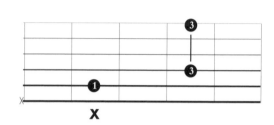

X

Gmin6

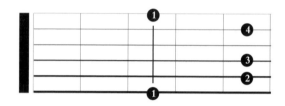

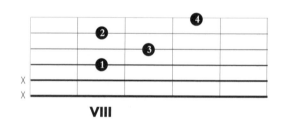

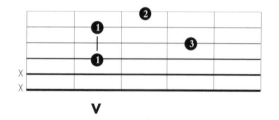

V

VIII

G6add9

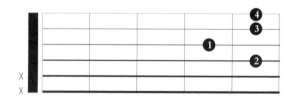

G6add9

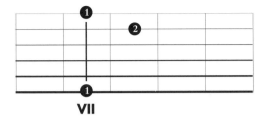

VII

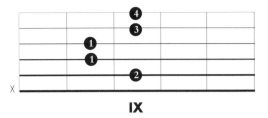

IX

G7

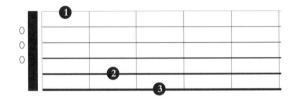

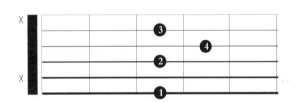

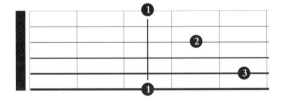

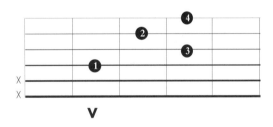

V

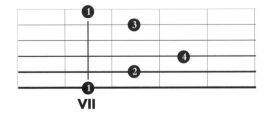

VII

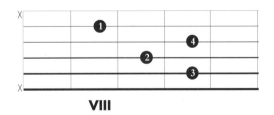

VIII

G7

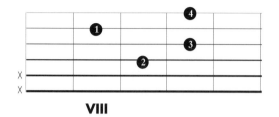

VIII

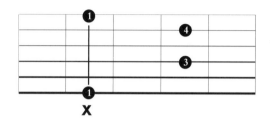

X

Gmin7

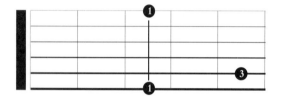

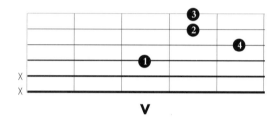

V

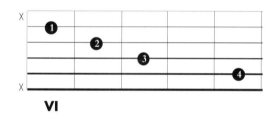

VI

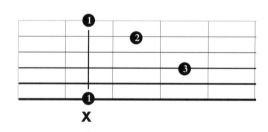

X

Gmin7/♭5

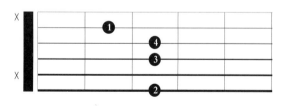

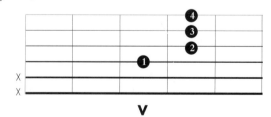

V

Gmin7/♭5

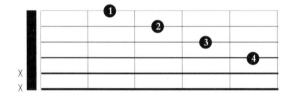

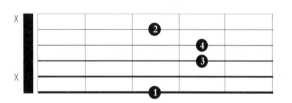

Gmaj7

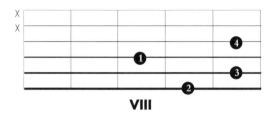

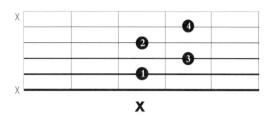

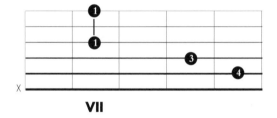

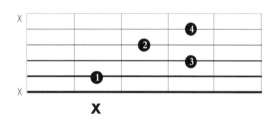

Gdim7

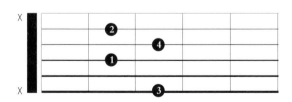

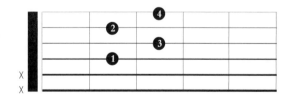

Gdim7

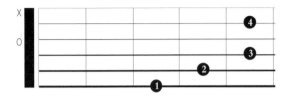

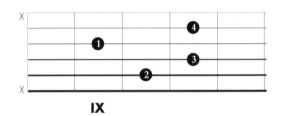

G7/#5

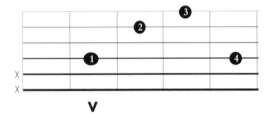

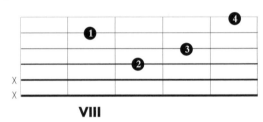

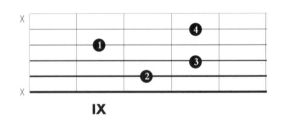

Gmin/maj7

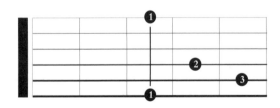

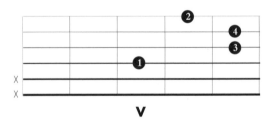

Gmin/maj7

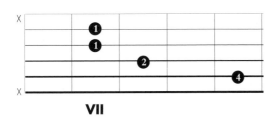

VII

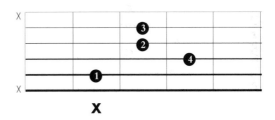

X

G7sus

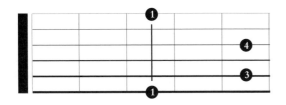

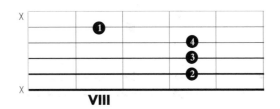

VIII

Gmin7sus

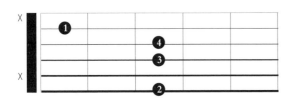

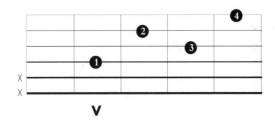

V

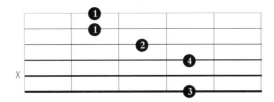

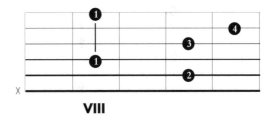

VIII

G9

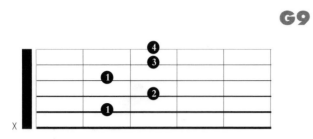

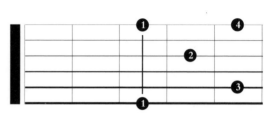

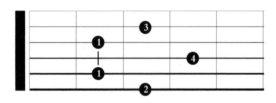

VII

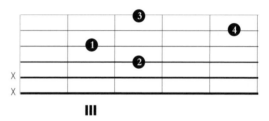

IX

Gmaj7/9

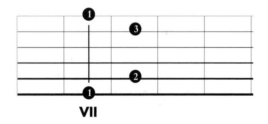

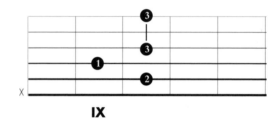

III

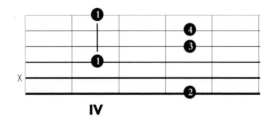

IV

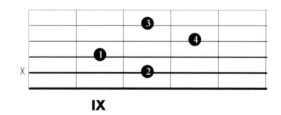

IX

Gmin9

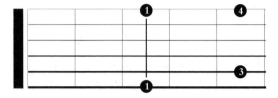

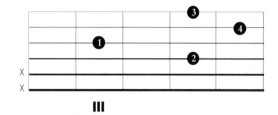

III

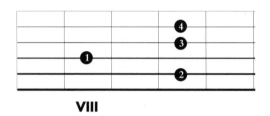

VIII

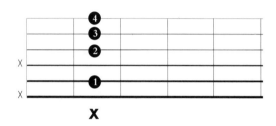

X

G11

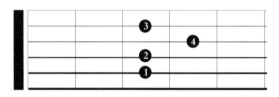

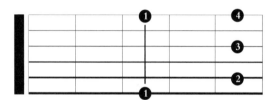

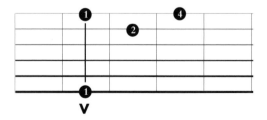

V

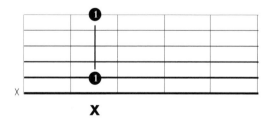

X

G13

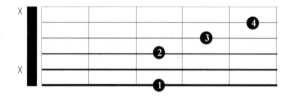

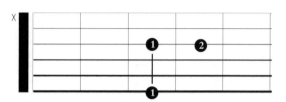

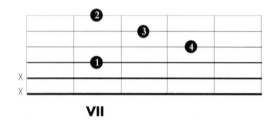

VII

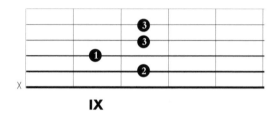

IX

Chords Built on
G♯ or A♭
(Sol♯/La♭)

G#Major or Ab Major

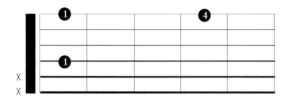

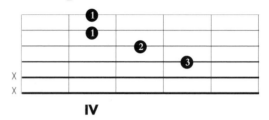

IV

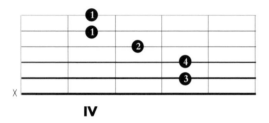

IV

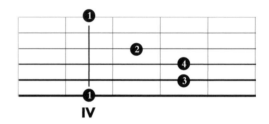

IV

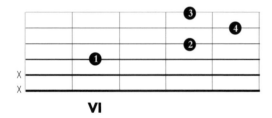

VI

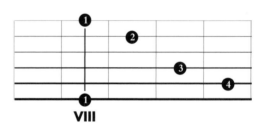

VIII

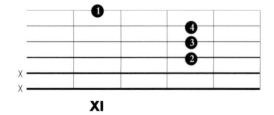

XI

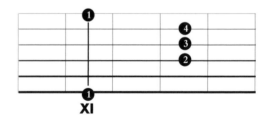

XI

G#Minor or A♭ Minor

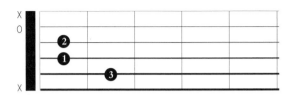

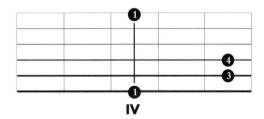

IV

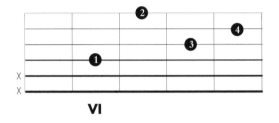

VI

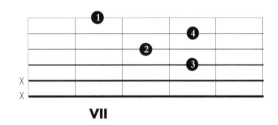

VII

G#aug or A♭aug

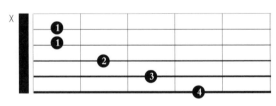

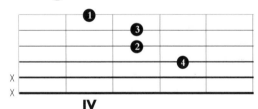

IV

G#6 or A♭6

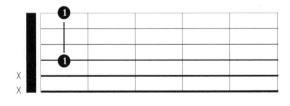

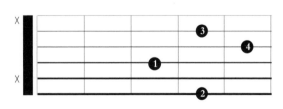

G#6 or Ab6

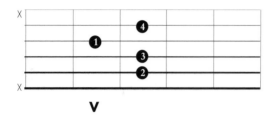

V

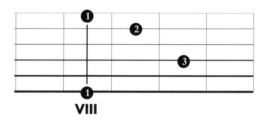

VIII

G#min6 or Abmin6

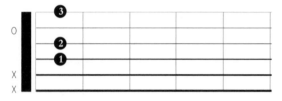

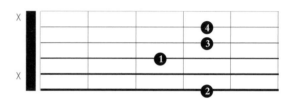

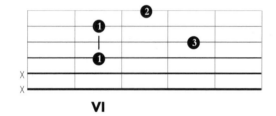

VI

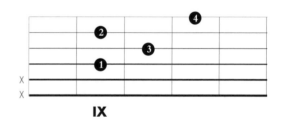

IX

G#6add9 or Ab6add9

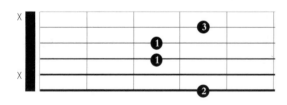

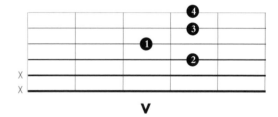

V

G#6add9 or A♭6add9

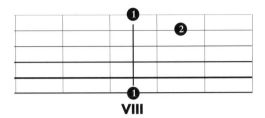

VIII

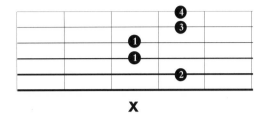

X

G#7 or A♭7

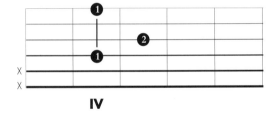

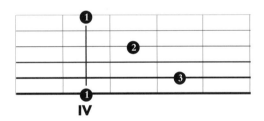

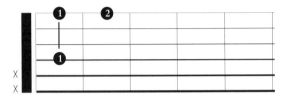

IV

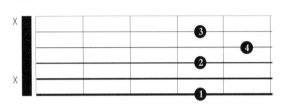

IV

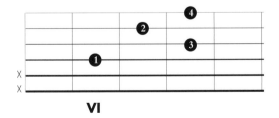

VI

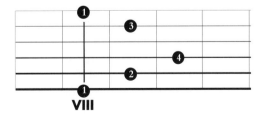

VIII

G#7 or Ab7

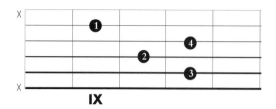

IX

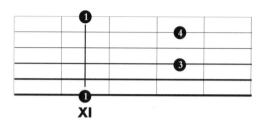

XI

G#min7 or Abmin7

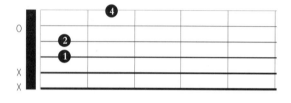

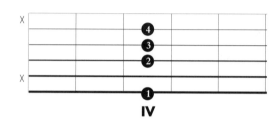

IV

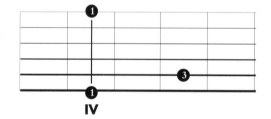

IV

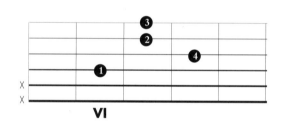

VI

G#min7/b5 or Abmin7/b5

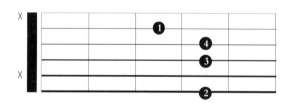

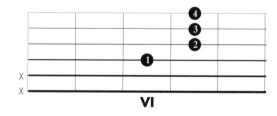

VI

G#min7/b5 or Abmin7/b5

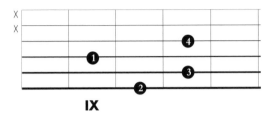

IX

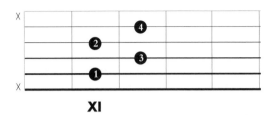

XI

G#maj7 or Abmaj7

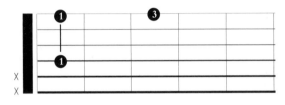

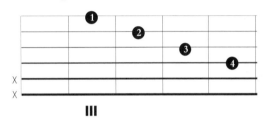

III

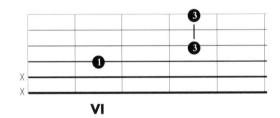

VI

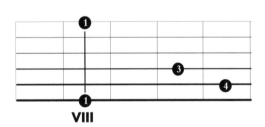

VIII

G#dim7 or Abdim7

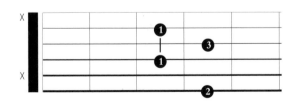

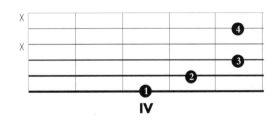

IV

G#dim7 or A♭dim7

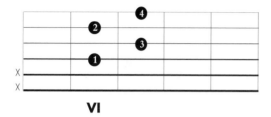

VI

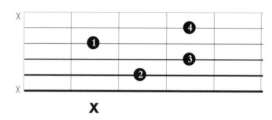

X

G#7/#5 or A♭7/#5

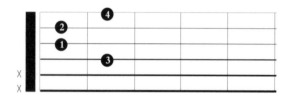

VI

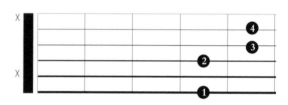

IX

G#min/maj7 or A♭min/maj7

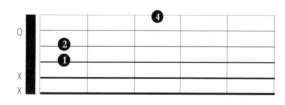

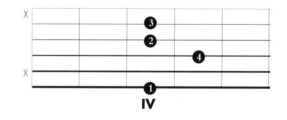

IV

G#min/maj7 or Abmin/maj7

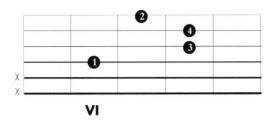

VI

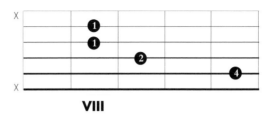

VIII

G#7sus or Ab7sus

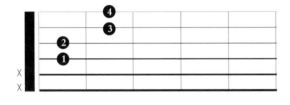

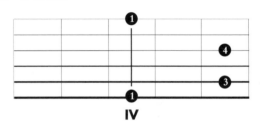

IV

G#min7sus or Abmin7sus

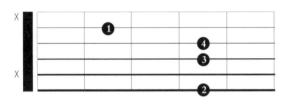

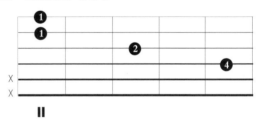

II

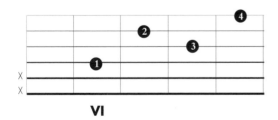

VI

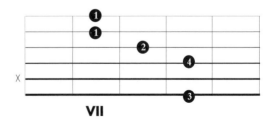

VII

G#9 or Ab9

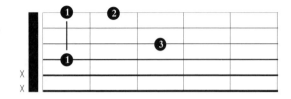

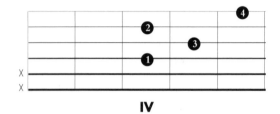

IV

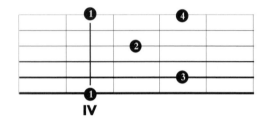

IV

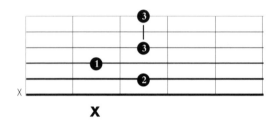

X

G#major7add9 or Abmajor7add9

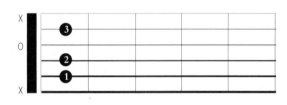

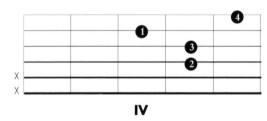

IV

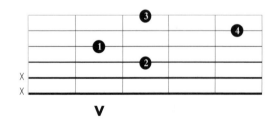

V

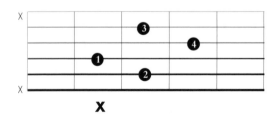

X

G#min9 or Abmin9

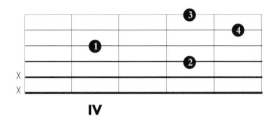

IV

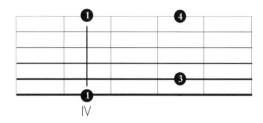

IV

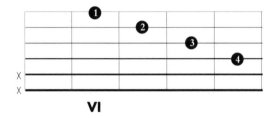

VI

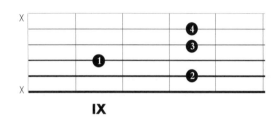

IX

G#11 or Ab11

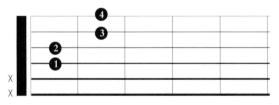

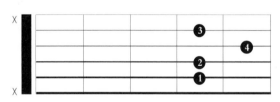

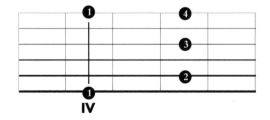

IV

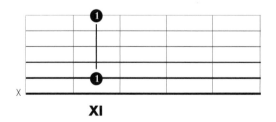

XI

G#13 or Ab13

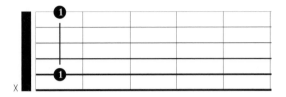

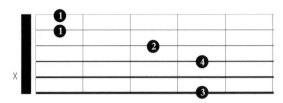

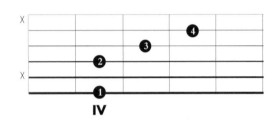

IV

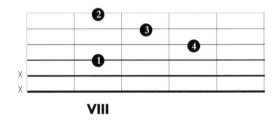

VIII

Chords Built on
A (La)

A Major

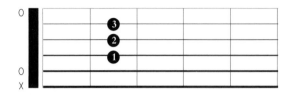

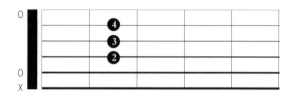

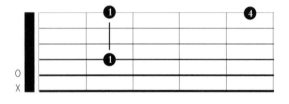

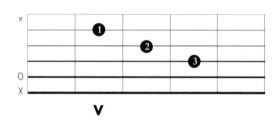

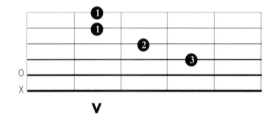

V

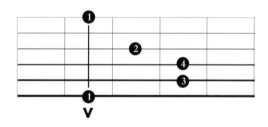

V

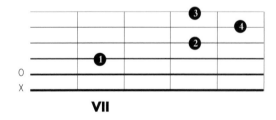

VII

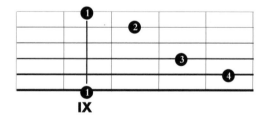

IX

A Minor

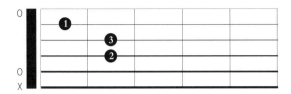

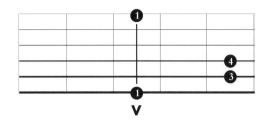

V

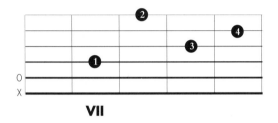

VII

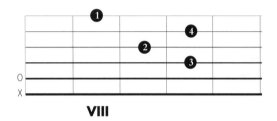

VIII

Aaug

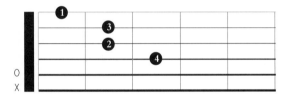

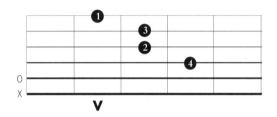

V

A6

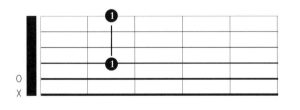

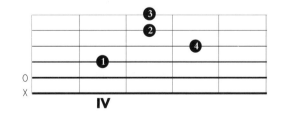

IV

A6

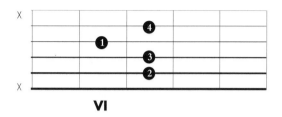

VI

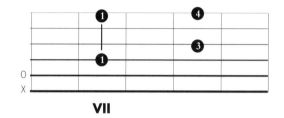

VII

Amin6

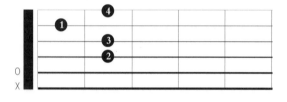

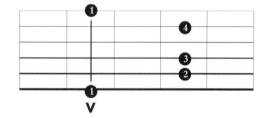

V

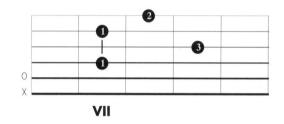

VII

A6add9

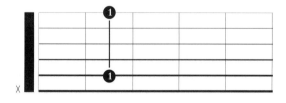

A6add9

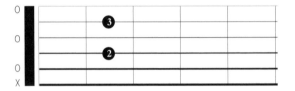

VI

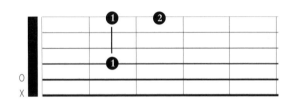

IX

A7

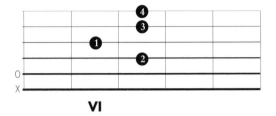

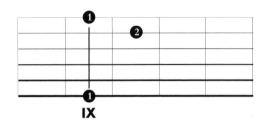

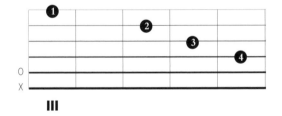

III

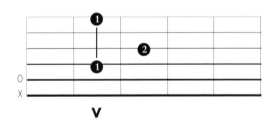

V

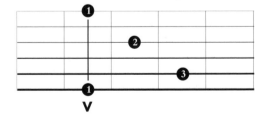

V

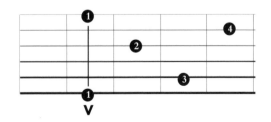

V

A7

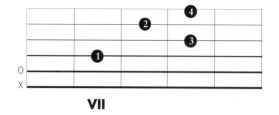

VII

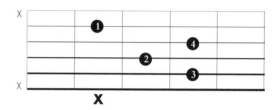

X

Amin7

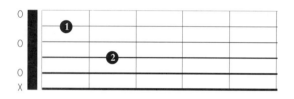

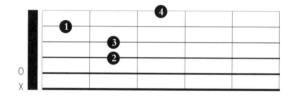

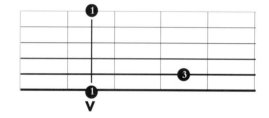

V

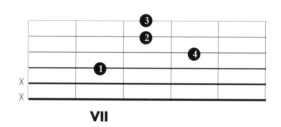

VII

Amin7/♭5

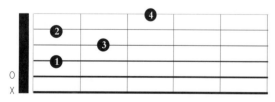

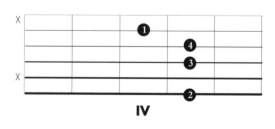

IV

Amin7/♭5

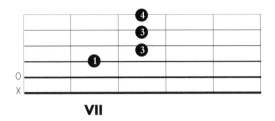

VII

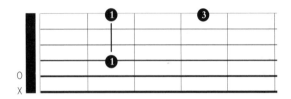

X

Amaj7

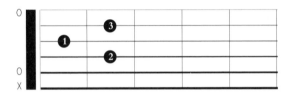

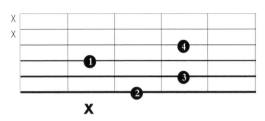

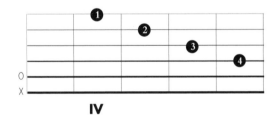

IV

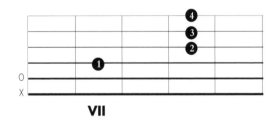

VII

Adim7

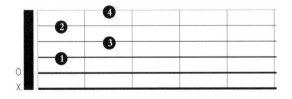

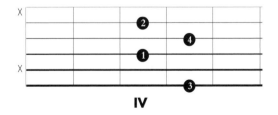

IV

Adim7

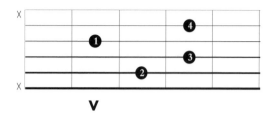

V

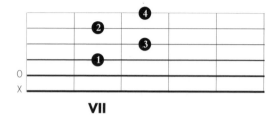

VII

A7/#5

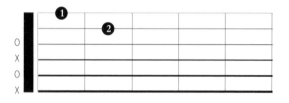

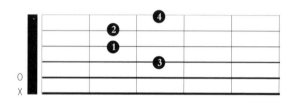

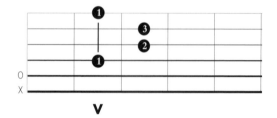

V

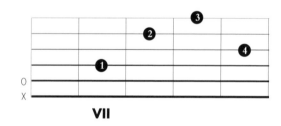

VII

Amin/maj7

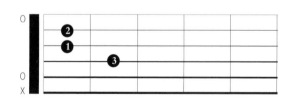

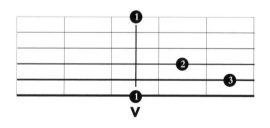

V

Amin/maj7

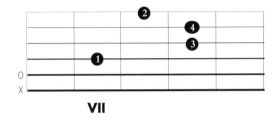

VII

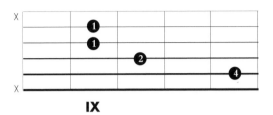

IX

A7sus

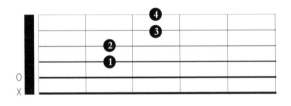

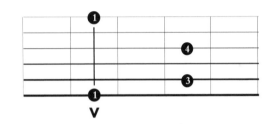

V

Amin7sus

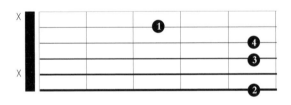

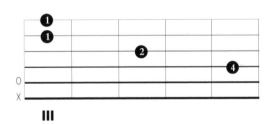

III

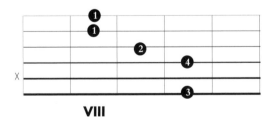

VIII

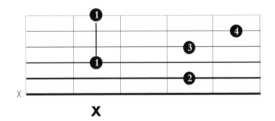

X

A9

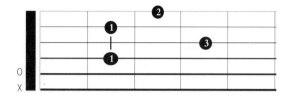

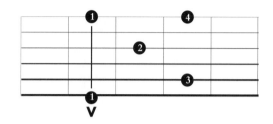

V

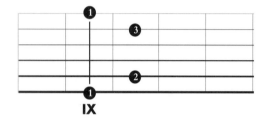

IX

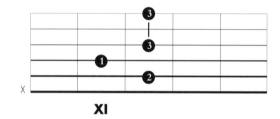

XI

Amaj7add9

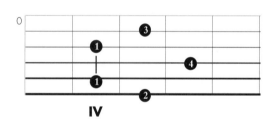

IV

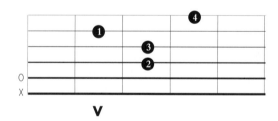

V

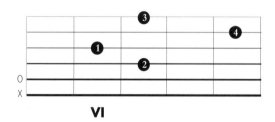

VI

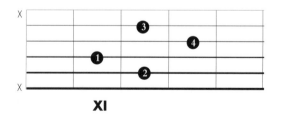

XI

Amin9

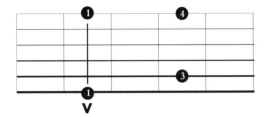

V

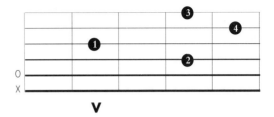

V

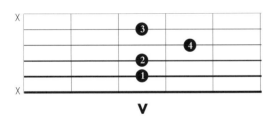

VIII

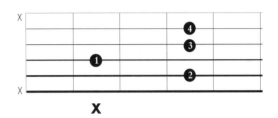

X

A11

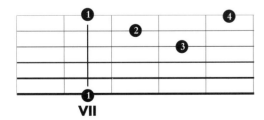

V

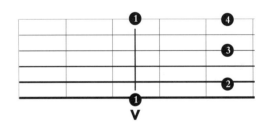

V

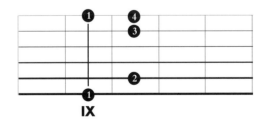

VII

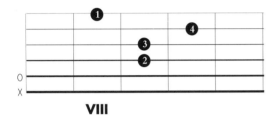

IX

A13

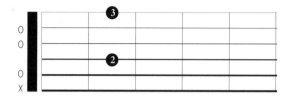

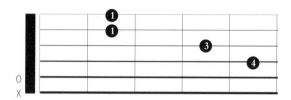

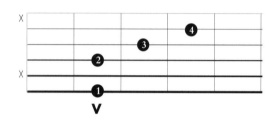

V

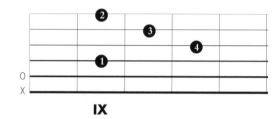

IX

Chords Built on
B♭ (Tib)

B♭ Major

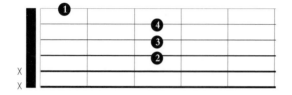

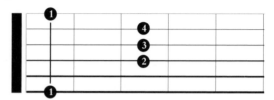

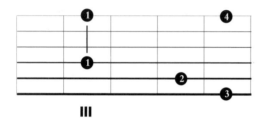

III

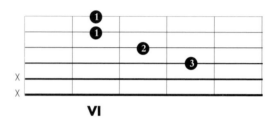

VI

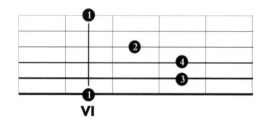

VI

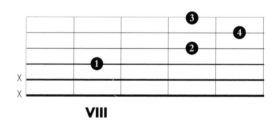

VIII

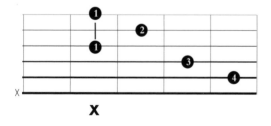

X

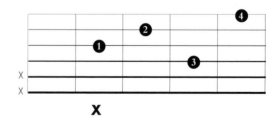

X

B♭ Minor

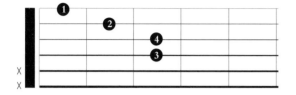

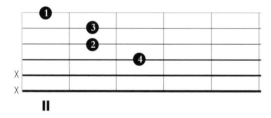

VI   IX

B♭aug

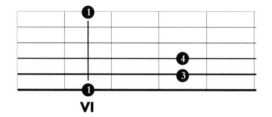

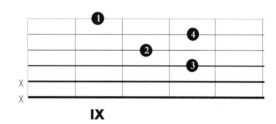

II   VII

B♭6

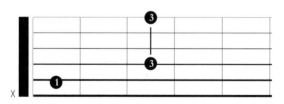

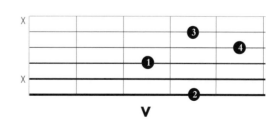

V

B♭6

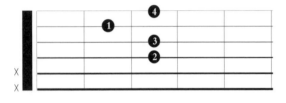

V

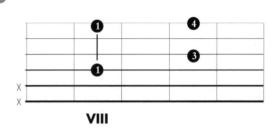

VIII

B♭min6

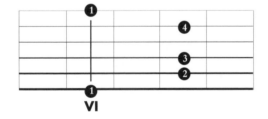

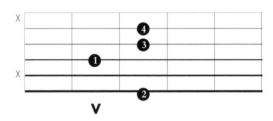

V

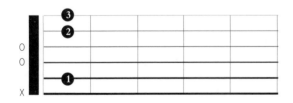

VI

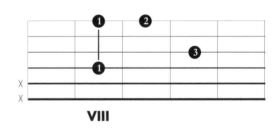

VIII

B♭min6add9

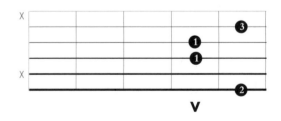

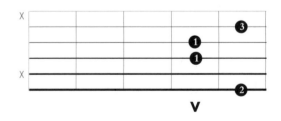

V

B♭min6add9

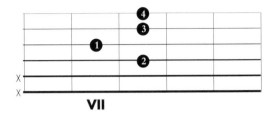

VII

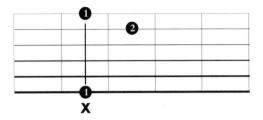

X

B♭min7

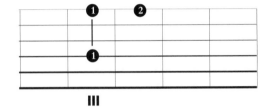

III

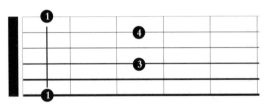

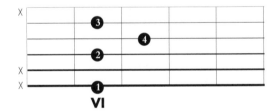

VI

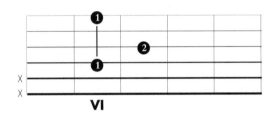

VI

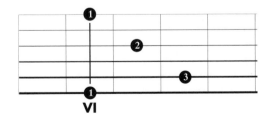

VI

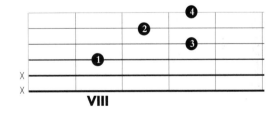

VIII

B♭7

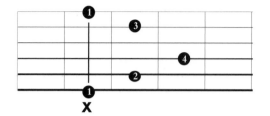

X

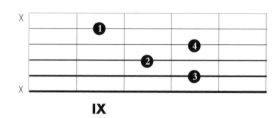

IX

B♭min7

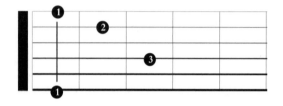

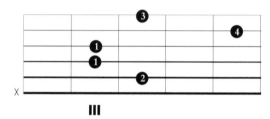

III

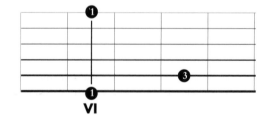

VI

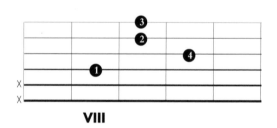

VIII

B♭min7/♭5

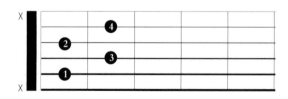

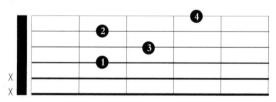

B♭min7/♭5

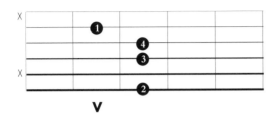

V

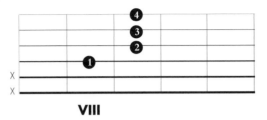

VIII

B♭maj7

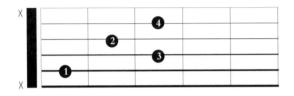

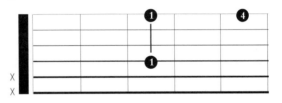

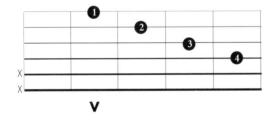

V

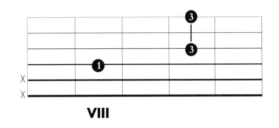

VIII

B♭dim7

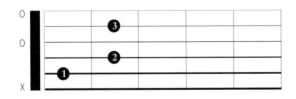

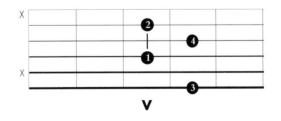

V

B♭dim7

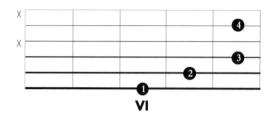

VI

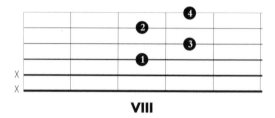

VIII

B♭7/#5

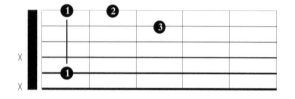

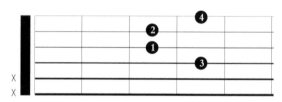

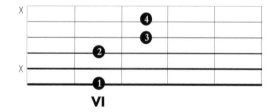

VI

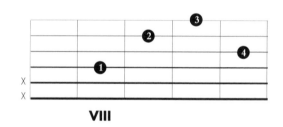

VIII

B♭min/maj7

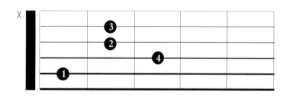

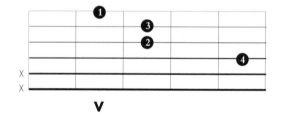

V

B♭min/maj7

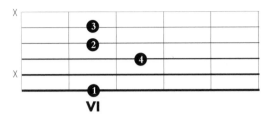

VI

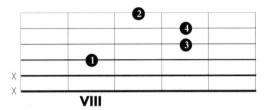

VIII

B♭7sus

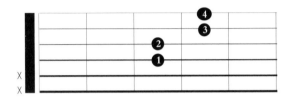

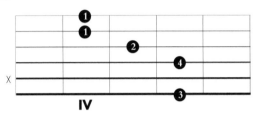

IV

B♭min7sus

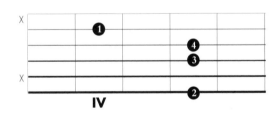

IV

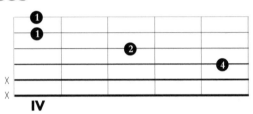

IV

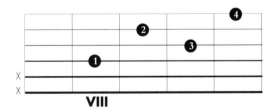

VIII

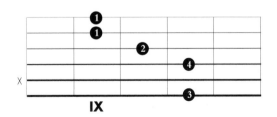

IX

B♭9

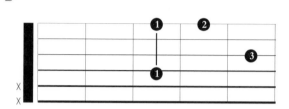

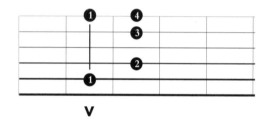

V

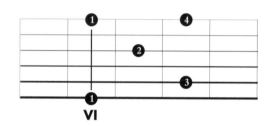

VI

B♭maj7add9

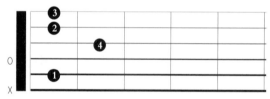

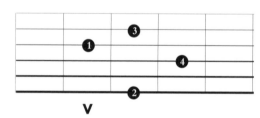

V

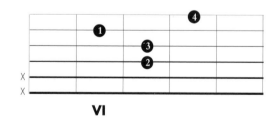

VI

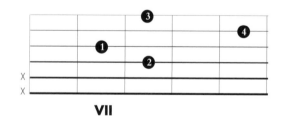

VII

B♭min9

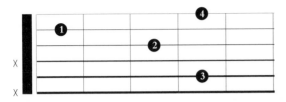

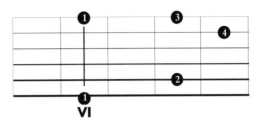
VI

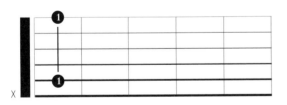

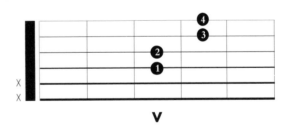
XI

B♭11

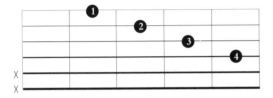
X

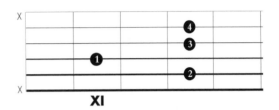
V

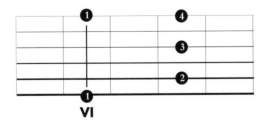
VI

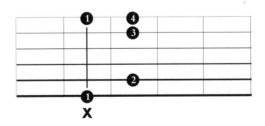
X

B♭13

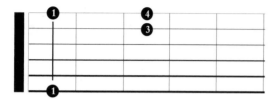

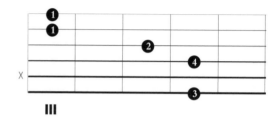

III

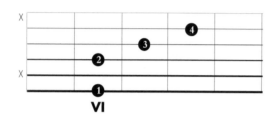

VI

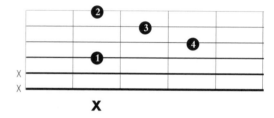

X

Chords Built on B (Ti)

B Major

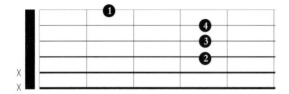

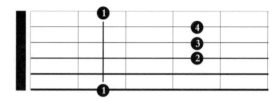

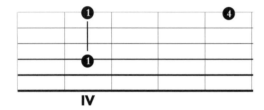

IV

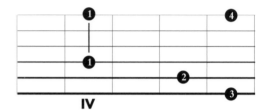

IV

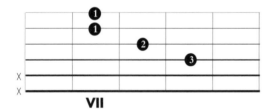

VII

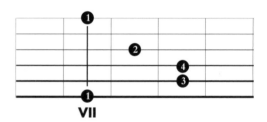

VII

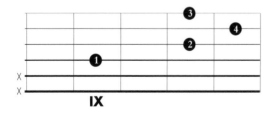

IX

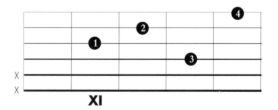

XI

B Minor

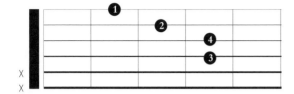

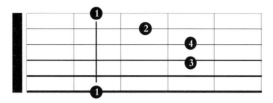

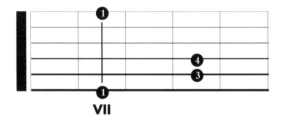

VII

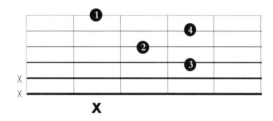

X

Baug

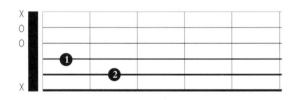

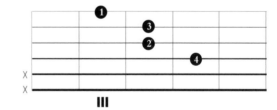

III

B6

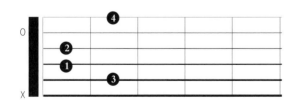

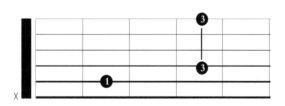

B6

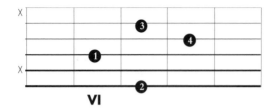

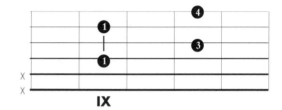

Bmin6

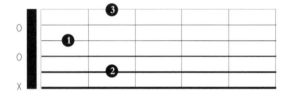

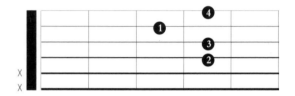

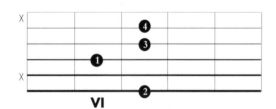

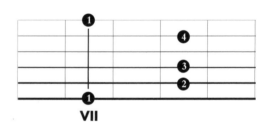

B6add9

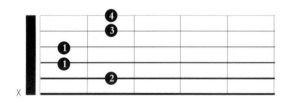

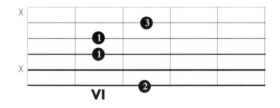

B6add9

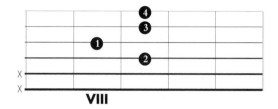

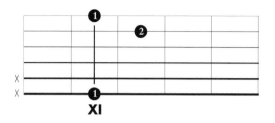

B7

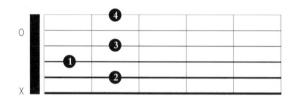

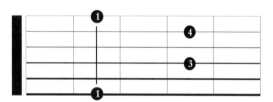

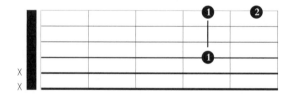

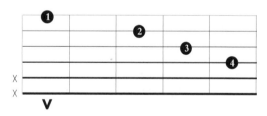

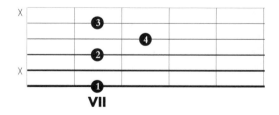

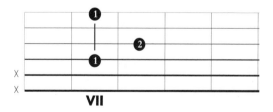

B7

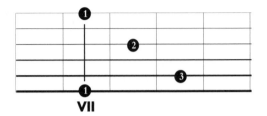

VII

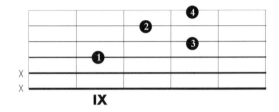

IX

Bmin7

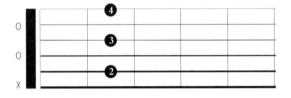

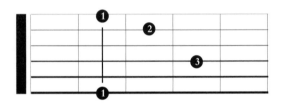

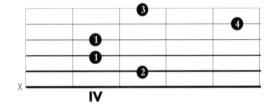

IV

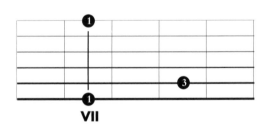

VII

Bmin7/♭5

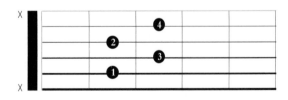

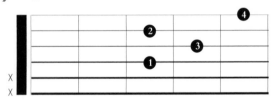

Bmin7/♭5

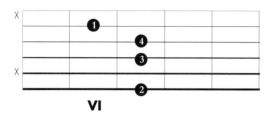

VI

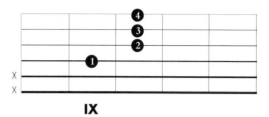

IX

Bmaj7

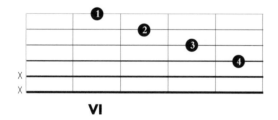

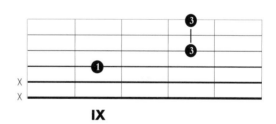

IV

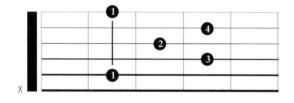

VI

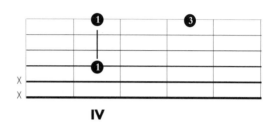

IX

Bdim7

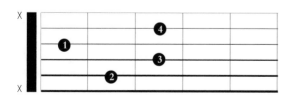

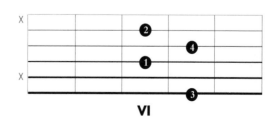

VI

Bdim7

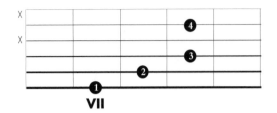

VII

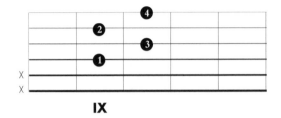

IX

B7/#5

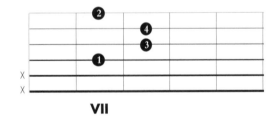

VII

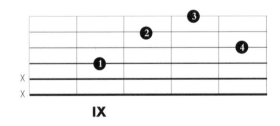

IX

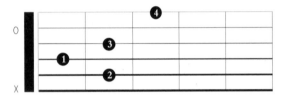

VII

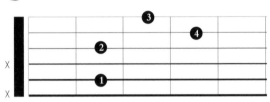

IX

Bmin/maj7

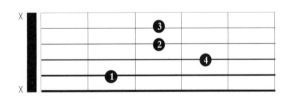

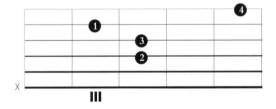

III

Bmin/maj7

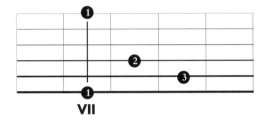

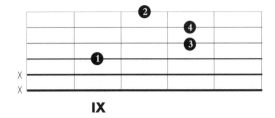

B7sus

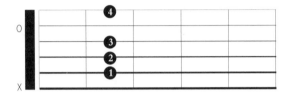

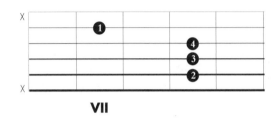

Bmin7sus

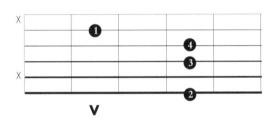

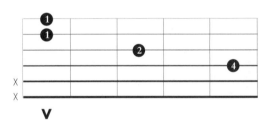

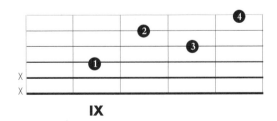

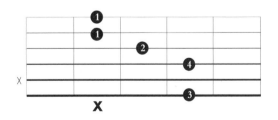

B9

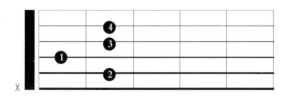

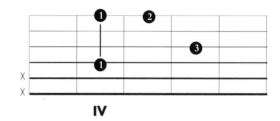

IV

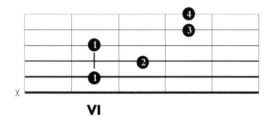

VI

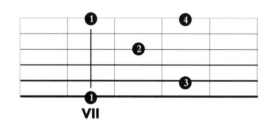

VII

Bmaj7add9

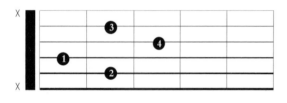

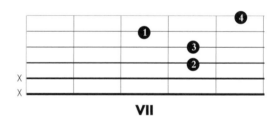

VII

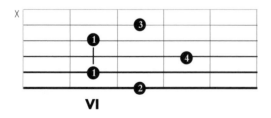

VI

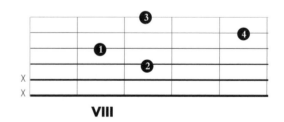

VIII

Bmin9

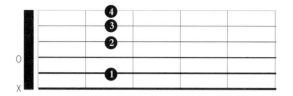
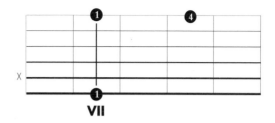

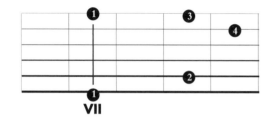
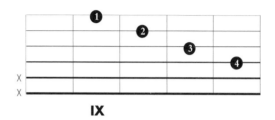

B11

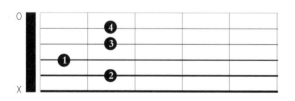
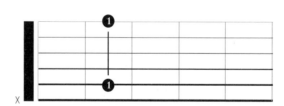

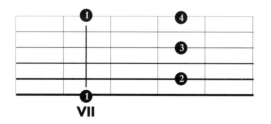
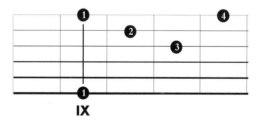

B13

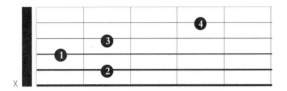

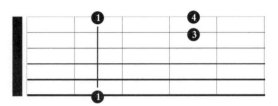

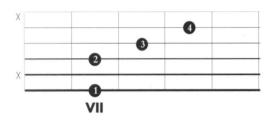

VII

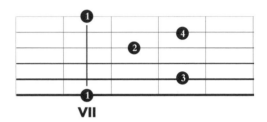

VII

Chapter 6
Using the Right Hand

In this chapter, we suggest ways to improve right-hand technique. We've minimized traditional musical staff notation to help clarify the technique.

Arpeggios should be executed both with fingers (classical style) and with the plectrum (the pick). Let's try to execute a simple arpeggio using the fingers. We'll play this sequence of open strings: the fifth, the third, the second, the third, the first, and again the third and the second. Each finger of the right hand corresponds to its own string.

For the Right Hand, Fingers Play These Strings

Fifth (A) string	thumb	T
Third (G) string	index finger	I
Second (B) string	middle finger	M
First (E) string	ring finger	R

Now let's match the movement of strings and fingers to a tempo.

To keep time, we apply the value of a quarter note to each beat, giving us two measures, each of 4/4 duration. Sounding the open strings in time to the measures indicated allows us to play the arpeggio. With the left hand in position on the fingerboard, let's now try to play an arpeggio using the simple **C Major** chord.

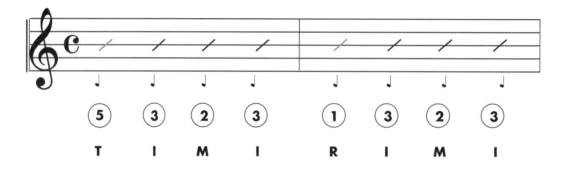

Here's the sequence of notes.

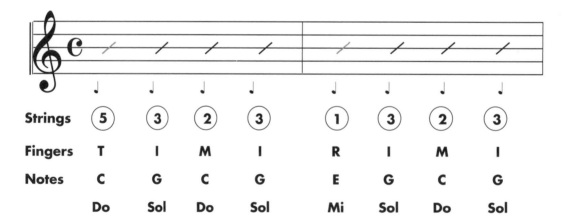

When these notes are written on the staff, they look like this.

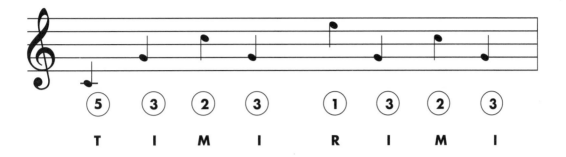

You can also play these notes with a pick (plectrum).

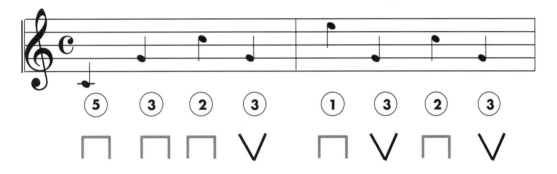

Use the pick (plectrum) or the appropriate finger(s) for the musical exercises on pp. 280–281.

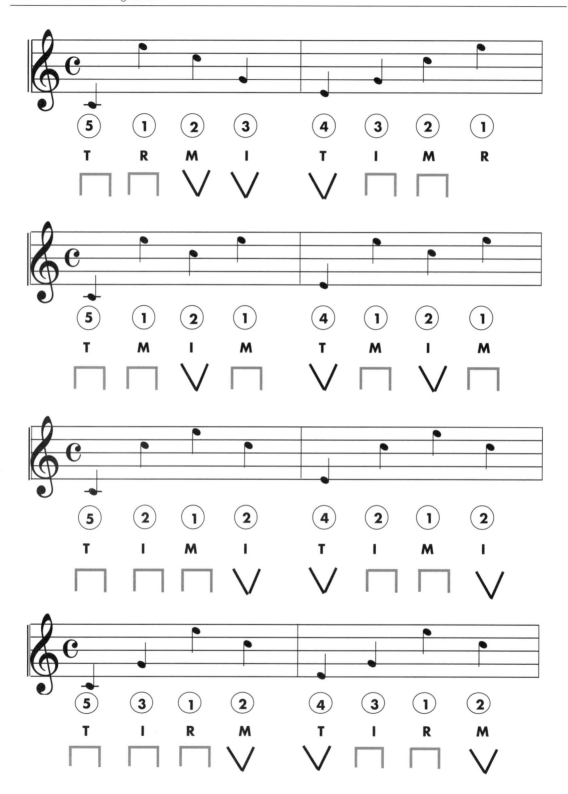

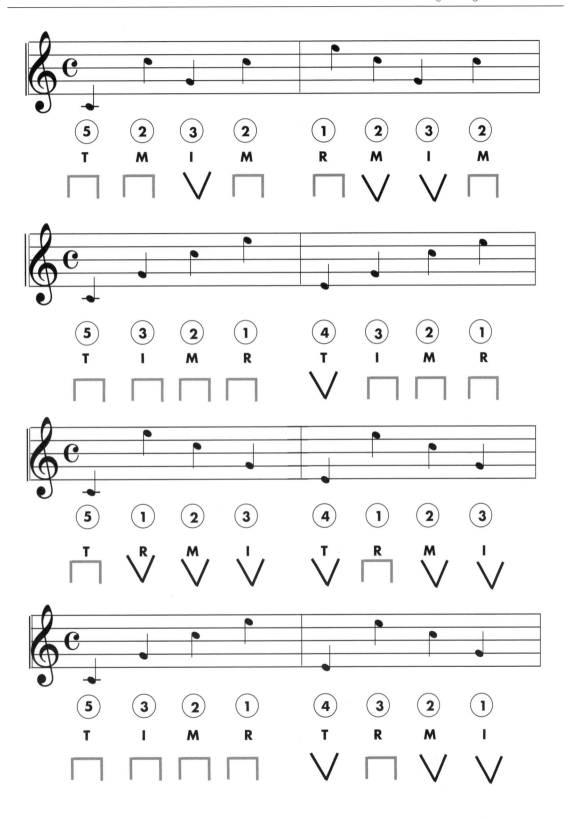

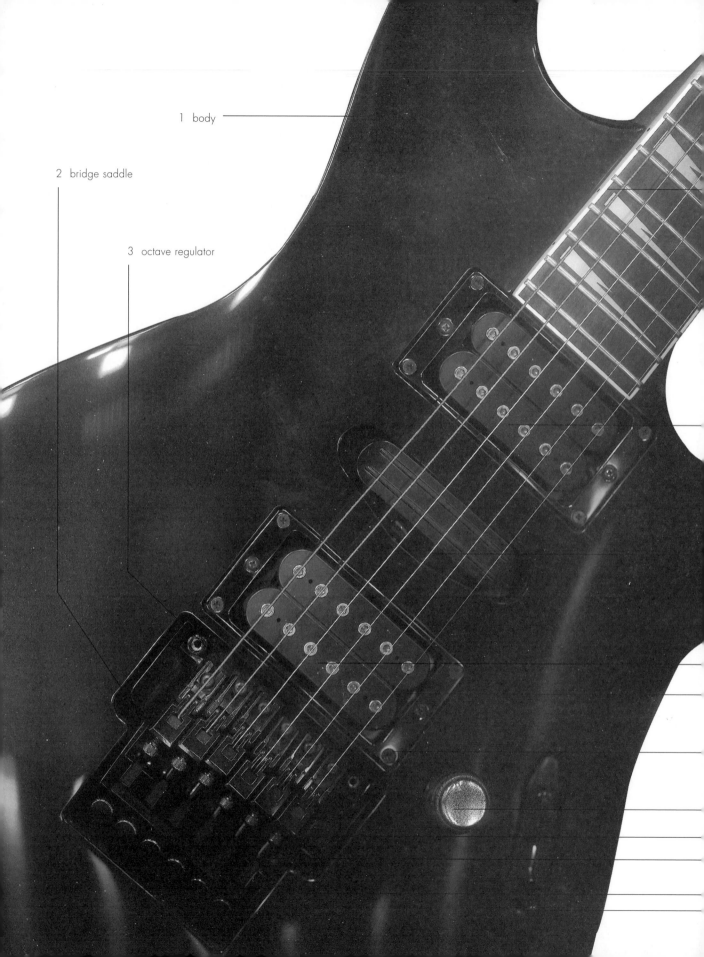

1 body

2 bridge saddle

3 octave regulator

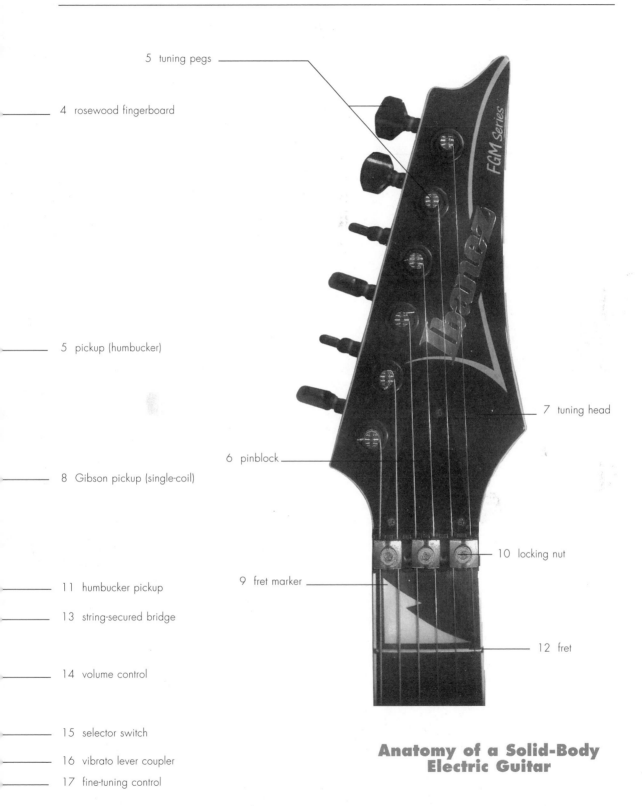

5 tuning pegs

4 rosewood fingerboard

5 pickup (humbucker)

8 Gibson pickup (single-coil)

11 humbucker pickup

13 string-secured bridge

14 volume control

15 selector switch

16 vibrato lever coupler

17 fine-tuning control

18 output socket

19 tone control knob

7 tuning head

6 pinblock

10 locking nut

9 fret marker

12 fret

Anatomy of a Solid-Body Electric Guitar

The photo (*left*) illustrates a *bending* execution carried out with the index finger. You may also use other fingers—the index, middle, ring, and pinky (little)—to carry out this movement. *Bending* means raising the intonation of the notes being played by "stretching" the strings upward, toward the player.

Practice and repeat these techniques to help you achieve good intonation.

In fingering scales (*photo right*), it's important to play with all four fingers of the left hand. During "solos" especially, and when improvising, train yourself to use the correct fingering.

When playing a chord, transpose it chromatically into all twelve keys; this is a good mnemonic exercise for learning the different positions.

Learn to use your guitar to help you refine your sense of pitch.

Practice arpeggios with the fingers of your right hand (*photo right*); then do the same with the pick. If using a plectrum, always remember to use an alternating stroke.

For *tapping*, use the right hand on the fingerboard in a percussive manner (*photo left*).

Try to "double" the sound of a note already being played by tapping on it slightly with one finger of the right hand.

Index